Ordeal of Change

Ordeal of Change

The Southern Utes and Their Neighbors

FRANCES LEON QUINTANA

WITH AN AFTERWORD BY RICHARD O. CLEMMER

ALTAMIRA
PRESS

A Division of
ROWMAN & LITTLEFIELD PUBLISHERS, INC.
Walnut Creek • Lanham • New York • Toronto • Oxford

ALTAMIRA PRESS
A division of Rowman & Littlefield Publishers, Inc.
1630 North Main Street, #367
Walnut Creek, CA 94596
www.altamirapress.com

Rowman & Littlefield Publishers, Inc.
A wholly owned subsidary of The Rowman & Littlefield Publishing Group, Inc.
4501 Forbes Boulevard, Suite 200
Lanham, MD 20706

PO Box 317
Oxford
OX2 9RU, UK

The textual numbering of references to endnotes employed in this work follows the format widely used in the physical sciences. Within each chapter, every citation is given a unique number, eliminating duplication of references while ensuring their integrity.

British Library Cataloguing in Publication Information Available

Library of Congress Cataloging-in-Publication Data

Quintana, Frances Leon.
  Ordeal of change : the southern Utes and their neighbors / by Frances Leon Quintana ; with an afterword by Richard O. Clemmer.
     p. cm.
  Includes bibliographical references and index.
  ISBN 0-7591-0709-2 (cloth : alk. paper) — ISBN 0-7591-0710-6 (pbk. : alk. paper)
  1. Ute Indians—History. 2. Ute Indians—Government relations. 3. Ute Indians—Land tenure. 4. Indian reservations—United States—History. 5. United States—Race relations. 6. United States—Politics and government. I. Title.

E99.U8Q85 2004
979.004'974576—dc22   2004012175

Printed in the United States of America

♾™ The paper used in this publication meets the minimum requirements of American National Standard for Information Sciences—Permanence of Paper for Printed Library Materials, ANSI/NISO Z39.48–1992.

Dedication

This study is dedicated to the memory of

- my faculty advisor, Professor Omer C. Stewart of the University of Colorado at Boulder. He introduced me to the Southern Utes and to their arduous and ultimately successful struggle to hold on to their identity in the face of Anglo-American hegemony,

- Professor Gordon Hewes, who was my teacher and shared with me a portion of his vast knowledge,

- Euterpe Taylor and her mother Kitty Cloud, Ute leaders both inspired by an unequaled devotion to their people, and

- my beloved husband, Miguel Felipe Quintana, who tenderly passed on to me his warm appreciation of his Southern Ute neighbors.

Contents

Figures

Abbreviations

ARCIA   *The Annual Report of the Commissioner of Indian Affairs* to the Secretary of the Interior including the Annual Reports of Indian Agents/Superintendents, Report of Board of Indian Commissioners and Indian Legislation passed by Congress. Commissioners' Annual Reports cited in this book include those of 1877, 1880, 1890, 1893, 1896, 1897, 1899, and 1900. Southern Ute Agents' annual reports cited are those of Henry Page (1880), Warren Patten (1884), Christian Stollsteimer (1885, 1887), Major H. B. Freeman (1893), and David Day (1895, 1896). These documents were published by Washington, D.C.: Government Printing Office.

BIA   Bureau of Indian Affairs

CCC   Civilian Conservation Corps

CETA   Comprehensive Education and Training Act

FRC   *Records of Southern Ute Agency, 1877-1952.* National Archives No. RG 75, Federal Records Center, Denver, Colorado

IRA   Indian Reorganization Act

NAGPRA   Native American Graves Protection and Repatriation Act

SUCAP   Southern Ute Community Action Program

Preface

This book details the ordeal undergone by the Southern Ute Indians following the American conquest of their ancestral lands. The first eight chapters cover the period from 1877, when the Utes were first confined to the reservation, until 1926. During this period, the Utes suffered profound privation. Tribal numbers plummeted. Indeed, the policy of the federal government was to destroy the tribe through forced assimilation. Failures to deliver promised rations and chicanery with individual financial accounts contributed to misery and decline.

The book is divided into four sections. The first section is comprised of four chapters, covering 1877-1926, which explore the issues of forcible relocation of Indians (Removal), the division of lands into individual holdings (Allotment), the issues of land and water usage that arose from allotment and how conflicting visions of administrators affected the preceding issues. These issues, which are fully exposed in the documents available in the Federal Records Center, are later shown to provide a firm foundation on which to analyze the nature of changes in Ute life. The next section is a brief statistical survey demonstrating the impact on demographic and economic outcomes. The next section analyzes these data and the final section, an Afterword by Professor Richard O. Clemmer, follows developments from 1926 to the present.

In the last two decades, the economic fortunes of the Ute tribe have greatly improved. Thanks to disciplined exploitation of mineral rights, especially of the rich oil and gas deposits on the reservation, and to development of the tourist industry, especially through a casino in Ignacio, the Ute tribe has moved onto sound financial footing. The Afterword provided by Dr. Clemmer, based on his recent work as an employee of the Southern Utes, will show, I think, that despite years under conditions that all but exterminated this small tribe, the Southern Utes have entered a new era of tribal life that promises a brilliant future. That future seems assured by the emergence of a generation of young tribal scholars who intend to re-examine the history of their people for the benefit of future generations. I hope that this book can contribute toward that objective.

One final development deserves comment. In 1996, indigenous plaintiffs filed and now have won a lawsuit against the Department of the Interior alleging gross abuses of tribal funds. At this writing, the presiding judge has ordered the Interior Department to attempt an accounting back to 1887. Tribes may ultimately be repaid billions of dollars in misappropriated funds. The present work includes information supportive of plaintiff's claims that, through negligence or malice, tribal funds may have been systematically looted under the aegis of the United States government. If this work can in any way help to redress these wrongs, it will make the long road from research to publication well worth it.

Acknowledgments

To Dr. Joel Swadesh, whose filial kindness is matched only by his skill with a Macintosh, for organizing my manuscript,

to Mr. James Hopkins, who once again has donated his labor and skill to the making of maps for this book,

and to Mrs. Liliosa Padilla and her daughters for a final proofreading.

Chapter 1
The Crucible

The 1870s ushered in a period of coercive change imposed by the government of the United States upon the lives of hunting-gathering Indians of the Plains and Rocky Mountains. The federal government sought to hem in the wide-ranging equestrian-nomadic tribes, including the scattered bands of Ute Indians whose exclusive domain stretched across western Colorado and eastern Utah (see map 1.1). In 1877, the three southern bands of Wiminuch, Muwach and Kapota Utes were assigned to an Indian agency located on the Pine River (Río de los Pinos) of southwestern Colorado where the town of Ignacio now stands. Successive treaties had whittled down their acknowledged territory to a narrow slice of southwestern Colorado, stretching from the San Juan River Valley westward to the Colorado-Utah border (see map 1.2). The Utes were forced to vacate their vast mountain territories by an aggressive flood of gold and silver prospectors and homesteaders who were permitted to displace them. The Brunot Agreement affirmed to the Utes the right to hunt and gather wild plants on the lands they had ceded but in fact they could only do so at the peril of their lives.

During the first fifty years of reservation life, from 1877 to 1926, the Utes were subjected to a policy which, while anticipating the eventual disappearance of all Native Americans, sought to "smoothe the dying pillow" while teaching these reluctant wards of the government to become as much like white Anglo-Saxon citizens as possible, in everything except the enjoyment of full citizen rights.

Described by Secretary of the Interior Carl Schurz in his 1877 Annual Report,[1] the main features of the policy were to be as follows:

1) The government must maintain good faith with the Indians by promising them only what could and would be fulfilled.
2) The hunting economy of the Indians must be discouraged: "When the Indians cease to be hunters, they will in a great measure cease to be warriors." To accomplish this, their supply of arms and ammunition must be reduced and their ponies must be exchanged for cattle.

3) To replace the Indians' hunting economy, a gradual transition to farming and cattle-raising must be promoted. Adequate reservation lands for such enterprise should be assured.

4) For tribes more adaptable to a pastoral way of life, agricultural training could play a subordinate role but should not be neglected.

5) Allotment of land in severalty should pave the way to civilization and citizenship, "the enjoyment and pride of the individual ownership of land being one of the most effective civilizing agents." Any head of a family who proved his capacity for self-support on his land over a period of years and who declared willingness to renounce his tribal relations should thereby become eligible for citizenship privileges.

6) Federal laws should be operative on the reservation and should be enforced by a system of Indian Police.

7) Education should be compulsory, preferably in boarding schools, with English as the sole language of instruction, thereby breaking the hold of aboriginal kin and society on the minds of the young.

8) Agency farms should be established, with skilled farmers in charge. Their function would be both to train the youth in schools and to visit and instruct Indian farmers.

9) Indian labor should be used wherever possible, as a part of Agency operation.

Carl Schurz was mindful of conflicting elements in the status of the Indians. They were nominally independent tribes whose power to make treaties with the federal government had barely been extinguished. At the same time, they were wards under the guardianship of that same government and in reality they were subjects under the forcible control of that government. Through his nine-point program, Schurz sought to stabilize the wardship side of Indian status in a direction pointing toward full citizenship. The assumption that went hand-in-hand with this goal was that those Indians who survived the ordeal of forcible change would have lost their own culture and would have no choice but to follow the dominant culture.

By 1926, the Muwach and Kapota segment of the Southern Utes, with headquarters in Ignacio, Colorado, had seemingly advanced in the direction sought by Schurz. They had accepted individual allotment of land in 1895, owned houses, engaged in some farming, had some schooling, and spoke some English. Superficially, their way of life resembled that of their non-Ute neighbors. Even this "advanced" segment of Utes, however, was far from being culturally assimilated to the Anglo-American way of life. Their preferred language and residence in tents, their relation to farming, their concepts of kinship, their love of mobility, and their general outlook remained distinctively Ute. In the eyes of Agency personnel and Anglo-American neighbors, they remained stubbornly, irritatingly, and obnoxiously Ute.

Most of the Wiminuch had refused land allotment, farming programs, and any concession to the assimilationist goal. They had withdrawn to a separate reservation in the Navajo Springs-Towaoc area near the Four Corners where Utah, Colorado, New Mexico, and Arizona meet. It must be added that some Muwach and Kapota opponents of allotment had joined them. Since the Utes had kinship ties that crossed band lines, such moves were not disruptive. In fact, Southern and Mountain Utes had similar ties with members of the Northern Ute bands, now pinned down on reservations in northeastern Utah.

The questions addressed in this book are: How did the Utes survive the first fifty years of reservation life, years during which they were constantly impeded from living as they had before, obliged to cope with a new set of rules imposed upon them? What conditions did they face and in what ways did these conditions change over the years? The answers to many of these questions are to be found in the records of the Southern Ute Agency, filed in the Federal Records Center in Denver, Colorado.

In 1959, Dr. Omer C. Stewart was my faculty advisor in the Graduate School Department of Anthropology at the University of Colorado. He offered me the job of organizing, analyzing, and filing the Southern Ute Agency records. At that time, he was gathering all available materials on the Utes in preparation for a government-funded research project in the Ignacio area (NIMH Grant No. 3M-9156), to be known as the Tri-Ethnic Project.

I worked at the Records Center in Denver (FRC) for the better part of a year, following the intricate filing code system in which employees of the Center patiently instructed me. Dr. Stewart published my file in his *Ethnohistorical Bibliography of the Ute Indians of Colorado*[2] as "Appendix A, Analysis of Records of the Southern Ute Agency, 1877 through 1952, National Archives RG 75." The FRC code numbers given in the Endnotes are the guide to locating the original documents at the Federal Records Center in Denver.

While filing those records, I began to compile a personal file on topics which struck me as extraordinarily significant. The file I made was limited to the first fifty years of Agency operation because, in the 1920s, new records disposal regulations led to the destruction of many documents, especially letters and informal interim reports. Although there are gaps in the earlier documentary record, largely due to the carelessness of Agency personnel, the records of the first fifty years reveal a great deal about relations, among the Utes themselves, between the Utes and the Agency and, most enlightening, between the Utes and various neighbors. Relations with the vast majority of Anglo-American neighbors were chilly, to say the least. Most of these neighbors wrote only to complain about and denounce the Utes. Most of the Anglos came from distant areas, had no previous acquaintance with Native Americans, and found them repulsive.

By contrast, the Hispanic neighbors were well acquainted with the Utes. Some of them had been specifically invited by the Utes to come and settle near them. A few were even invited by the Utes to use their grazing lands. Hispanic neighbors formed a balancing influence which provided alternatives to the draconian program of the Agency and Indian Office.

My perception of these contrasting relations was dramatically reinforced as soon as I began to do field research for the Tri-Ethnic Project starting in the summer of 1960. Portions of my field notes enlarge upon the narrative of the Agency records in this book. They owe a great deal to the recollections and perceptions of wise elders among the Utes, Hispanos, and some Anglos. The principal debt to their perceptions however, pervades my book *Pobladores: Hispanic Americans of the Ute Frontier*[3] (published in a second revised edition as *Los Primeros Pobladores: Hispanic Americans of the Ute Frontier*[4]). In that work, I have been able to document the relationship of Hispanic settlers with Ute trading partners back into the eighteenth century. Some of the eighteenth century settlers of the lower Chama Valley were direct ancestors of the Hispanos who settled south and east of the Southern Ute reservation.

In addition to Anglo and Hispanic neighbors of the Utes, Navajo, Jicarilla Apache, and Paiute residents of the area had an important role in the daily life of the Southern Utes. Some of them became members of the Southern Ute and/or Ute Mountain populations. In addition, certain Comanches and Kiowas from Oklahoma, a husband from Taos Pueblo, one from the San Juan Pueblo and, finally but not least, a versatile and talented African American became incorporated into Southern Ute society, each one enriching the cultural palette of Southern Ute life.

When I commenced my study, anthropological theory was tilted toward the idea of culture change as the product of assimilation to the dominant culture in a cross-cultural situation, or at least to the disintegration of traditional cultures faced with coercive conditions such as those the Southern Utes experienced. Among the few scholars who, at that time had formulated a different approach to culture contact and culture change, I was guided by Edward Spicer's analysis of the structure of contact relations in seventeenth century Yaqui-Jesuit experience in Sonora.[5] Even more, I was influenced by Melville Herskovits' observation that dominant-subordinate relationships between cultures do not necessarily lead either to assimilation or to cultural disintegration but rather to variability and complexity of cultural patterns.[6]

The Southern Utes did not assimilate nor did tribal culture disintegrate. Rather, by intelligence and hardy persistence, the Southern Utes succeeded in maintaining their tribal identity and prospering in the face of adversity. Some elements of the culture, such as shamanistic practices, may have been lost. Others, such as the Sun Dance and Bear Dance are increasingly the preserve of older Utes. The Southern Utes, however, have found means of preserving culture, notably through the establishment of a "Ute Academy." I hope that this study of United States federal hegemony over the Southern Utes in their first fifty years on the Pine River Reservation, supplemented by Professor Richard Clemmer's review of Ute progress since then, will convince readers of the persistence and elasticity of Ute culture over time.

Map 1.1. Ute Territory, Pre-U.S. Occupation
(Reproduced with permission from Stewart[7])

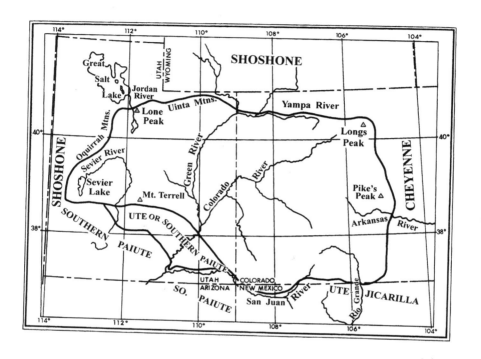

6

Map 1.2. Current Southern Ute Reservation
(by Frances Leon Quintana, with permission)

Chapter 2
The Context of Change

On April 17, 1877, a young Civil War veteran turned clergyman and farmer, Francis Weaver by name, received notice of his appointment as Indian Agent for the bands of Utes of Southern Colorado at an annual salary of $1,200 plus traveling expenses. He was instructed to proceed with dispatch to Santa Fe, and there to meet with Pueblo Agent Ben Thomas, who was temporarily in charge of the Utes. Together, they were to locate a site for a new Agency within the southern portion of the reservation, assigned to the Utes by the Treaty of 1868. It lay south of the mountainous San Juan mining region, relinquished in the Brunot Agreement of 1874.

Criteria for selection of the site were to be sufficiency of timber, water, and agricultural and grazing lands, also accessibility to "roads and routes of travel now existing or likely hereafter to be made and used." The final instructions were succinct: "When the Agency shall have been established, your next duty will be the gathering of the Indians who properly are embraced in it."[1] In a separate letter, Weaver was notified that he should erect temporary Agency buildings at a cost not to exceed $2,000.[2]

As Weaver proceeded to fulfill his first assignments, he had little idea as to the location and numbers of the Indians he was to relocate. About 307 of them, mainly Muwaches, were on the huge Maxwell Ranch near Cimarron, New Mexico. An unknown number of Kapotas and Wiminuches were being administered to along with the Jicarilla Apaches at Tierra Amarilla under the Abiquiu Agency, New Mexico. The total number of all Indians appearing irregularly at Abiquiu was guessed at around 900.[3] Nearly a year was to pass before Weaver was to meet with any considerable number of Muwaches and Kapotas. On his way northwest to the assigned reservation, however, Weaver happened on the camp of the Wiminuch leader, Ignacio, just east of the reservation line, and made his first uneasy acquaintance with Utes in June, 1877. Ignacio and his followers peremptorily demanded an Agency location on the Navajo River, barely within the eastern border of the reservation; they said this location had been promised them at a conference in Washington, and vowed that "they would never have anything to do with an agency located anywhere else; but it is believed that they were influenced to this course by interested parties . . . a few of that noble band of men who are always working 'entirely for the public good.'" Weaver, however, decided on a site on the Pine River, midway between the eastern extreme demanded by Ignacio and the western end of the reservation where a number of his Indians were located. In the Pine River (Río de los Pinos) Valley, he found adequate resources of water, timber, and agricultural and grazing lands, as well as easy access to all-season roads. The nearest sawmill was at some distance but so, providentially, was the nearest town (Animas City, later Durango), a raw mining community which could "act as a terrible demoralizer of any Indian Agency." Weaver predicted that the Utes could be brought to see the advantages of the location he had selected, despite their prejudices and the "forces of evil of other parties," but only with active cooperation from Washington: "These Indians have not been nearly so liberally treated as that portion of the tribe located at the northern end of the reservation; they have miserable clothing and tents and many of them live so far from their present source of supplies at Tierra Amarilla that they have not been able to draw their rations except at very long intervals." Weaver urged the prompt and liberal shipment of "all the annuity goods usually furnished Indians when it is desired to control them" and, in addition, adequate rations. The chiefs, he said, complained bitterly of "presents" promised to them in Washington several years back but not yet delivered.[3]

In the months which followed, Weaver had to reiterate with increasing urgency his request for shipment of supplies and annuity goods, long overdue. In August, he informed the Commissioner of Indian Affairs that when the Utes "clamored for shirts and blankets and asserted that for four years they had been cheated out of what had been promised," he could only appease them by assuring them "on the word of the honorable Commissioner that the shipments would arrive by September."[4] By December, the Utes were suffering from the cold and, being low on ammunition for hunting purposes, also from hunger.[4] Despite their hunger, word of contract supplies on the way inspired them to demand rations of mutton instead of beef.[5] In late December, many of the Utes moved south, on the trail of game driven out of the mountains by heavy snowfalls; they promised to return when the snow melted. Temporarily relieved of his troublesome charges, Weaver took the compassionate view that, "all things considered, these Utes have been very patient and bore their disappointment with commendable resignation."[6]

The Removal Issue

While Weaver was laboring to establish his little Agency on the Pine River, a matter was under consideration in Washington which, in one form or another, was to keep the Utes in a state of uncertainty for the next eighteen years: the question of removal. In his first Annual Report, newly appointed Commissioner of Indian Affairs Hayt promoted the view that the smaller tribes of the West should be concentrated in the Indian Territory of Oklahoma. This proposal would embrace the Indians of Colorado.[7] While Weaver was with much difficulty constructing a temporary Agency building and log issue house with adobe floors, a bill for removal of the Utes from Colorado was before Congress, and Hayt sent instructions to the young Agent to suspend his building work.[8] Long before the letter reached Weaver, however, the buildings were completed.

By mid-1878, a set of new terms for removal, to be negotiated by the Hatch Commission, proposed consolidation of all the Ute bands, both Northern and Southern, at an Agency to be located on or near the White River and the extinguishment of all rights of the Southern Utes to their reservation in Southwestern Colorado.[9] When General Hatch and his commissioners, the Hons. William Stickney and N. C. McFarland, placed this proposal before the Southern Utes, the Indians flatly refused to discuss consolidation with the Northern Utes. They stated that they did not wish to relinquish rights to their reservation but agreed to sell it in exchange for one which would include the headwaters of the Navajo, Blanco, San Juan, Piedra, and Pine rivers, provided they were first paid $80,000 which they claimed was already due them.[10]

The willingness of the Utes of southwestern Colorado to accept further removal was due to their growing awareness of the intention to make farmers of them, a prospect which they viewed with distaste. Weaver's exhortations on the virtues of farm labor were hardly keyed to the tastes of equestrian nomads, skilled and persistent hunters: "Their excessive indolence allows of no comparison," lamented Weaver, "and any improvement advanced upon their accustomed manner of life is so obnoxious that the simple broaching of the subject is sufficient to warrant their disgust. The men will do nothing and say that their fathers lived without work and why not they. The spirit of braggadocio sometimes manifests itself to a considerable extent among the men, some of whom yet hold out that they are the most powerful among the people of the earth. The women on the other hand are exceedingly backward and subject to all the work and drudgery imaginable. Upon them depends the care of whatever stock is possessed, as well also as the domestic affairs, in short of all their affairs."[11]

Disagreement with the aims and methods promoted by the Indian Bureau caused the Utes to vote, when given the opportunity to do so, for transfer of Indian Affairs from the Interior to the War Department. Transmitting the results of a consensus among the men, reported on by Aguila and Charley (also known as Buckskin Charley and, later, as Charles Buck) for the Muwaches, Tumpiatch and Severo for the Kapotas, and Passagouche and Alhandro for the Wiminuches, Weaver cited the following reasons given for the Indians' preference: under the War Department, they would receive their beef on the hoof rather than having it slaughtered by Agency personnel; they would not have to farm; they would "be as before—we want to be at peace with everybody and want no arguments."[12]

With the above in mind, the Utes continued to discuss removal of the Agency to a location much too mountainous for farming; yet in reality they did not desire to move. Weaver wrote:

> Considerable dissatisfaction exists concerning the removal of the Agency to the Rio Navajoe as was proposed to the Indians and agreed to in part when the Commissioner was here. I have kept quiet about this affair as I deemed it none of my business, but I cannot now but say that such removal will answer only as a subterfuge until another removal occurs. The vicinity of the Navajoe is "the coldes' place in creation" and the Indians cannot be held there during the winter season, but will roam south and east to the annoyance and loud condemnation of citizens. [13]

Although the foregoing proposals for removal of the Northern and Southern Utes to Oklahoma or to the White River and the Southern Ute counter-proposal for an Agency on the Navajo River were not carried through, schemes for removal continued with mounting pressure. The White River rebellion in 1879 created a sensation which inspired the Anglo-American settlers of the Four Corners area to intensify their demands for removal of the Southern Utes. Agent Stanley of the Los Pinos Agency, headquarters of the Uncompahgre Utes in the mountains between the San Luis Valley and the Gunnison River, confided to Southern Ute Agent Henry Page, "The White River trouble is a pigmy compared to the giant the newspapers try to make it,"[14] and, indeed, the Southern Utes in council had declared their neutrality in the White River controversy, although some of their members, relatives, and friends were involved. This did not deter the homesteading neighbors of the Southern Utes from demanding military protection against possible attack, and Col. J. Buell was sent to the mouth of the Animas River "to protect citizens of this valley against the hostile Utes."[15]

Not that the Utes did not have grounds for hostility against their intrusive neighbors. Already in 1878, Agent Weaver had estimated that thousands of cattle and sheep being illegally grazed on reservation lands were driving off the remaining game animals upon which the Utes still partly depended for subsistence. Meyers and Stollsteimer, for instance, had 2,000 cattle grazing on

Photo 2.1 Charles Buck, also known as Buckskin Charley
(J. E. Candelaria Collection, with permission)

Photo 2.2 Captain Severo Capote
(J. E. Candelaria Collection, with permission)

the Piedra;[16] it will be shown later how the conduct and policies of Christian Stollsteimer as Southern Ute Agent in 1885-1887 were seemingly influenced by his enjoyment of free pasture on reservation lands.

The White River furor and the heavily stimulated citizen alarm over the intentions of the Southern Utes resulted in a call by General Hatch of the Ute Commission to the new Ute Agent Henry Page. Instructions were to send Aguila and Buckskin Charley, chief and sub-chief of the Muwaches, to join a delegation of chiefs for renewed negotiations in Washington. Ouray was to head the delegation and Tapuche, chief of the Kapotas, was already with him in Alamosa, ready to leave on December 27.[17]

Upon receiving this news, the Wiminuches demanded that Ignacio and "several other influential Southern Utes" be included on the delegation, else the Wiminuches would not be bound by any agreements reached.[18] The revised delegation eventually reached Washington and Commissioner of Indian Affairs Marble in his Annual Report for 1880 advised that an agreement was signed July 29th and September 11th for removal from Colorado to "some other location."[19] This agreement appears to have been the one signed by a group of chiefs headed by Ignacio and Alhandro, in which the Southern Utes accepted removal to unoccupied agricultural lands along the La Plata Valley, possibly extending down into New Mexico.[20]

In the meantime, however, Congress had passed the Act of June 15, 1880, by which the Southern Utes relinquished title to their entire reservation except such lands as should be allotted in severalty. This Act was later to become the foundation of the Allotment Act of 1895. The proliferation of treaties and agreements which the Utes were induced to sign from 1849 on, many of them never ratified and others although ratified not carried out, resulted in confusion over many years as to their actual status. The Utes themselves appear to have remembered the terms of every treaty they had signed, but did not always know which ones were operative.

Talk of removal of the Southern Utes, coupled with encroachments upon their reservation lands, continued. In his 1881 Annual Report, Agent Page commented on the unsettling effect of the construction of the Denver and Rio Grande Railroad Line across the eastern section of the reservation, without "amicable arrangements" for compensating those Indians residing near the tracks. He added, "more or less trespassers on every side, the constant talk of removal, as well as the removal of the two other bands, the Uncompahgres and White Rivers, has kept these Indians in a constant state of uncertainty and excitement, which still continues to require constant care and watchfulness."[21]

The years between 1881 and 1885 marked the growth of an attitude on the part of some of the Utes' neighbors that an Indian had no rights that a white man was bound to respect. Here is some characteristic correspondence from irate citizens in Pagosa Springs: E. T. Walker complained to Colorado Governor Pitkin, who passed the letter on to Commissioner of Indian Affairs Price, who referred the matter to Agent Warren Patten, that the Utes were camping off the reservation near Pagosa Springs, hunting, "loafing" and presumably stealing. Walker wrote: "That hideous old cuss George Washington who assumes to be a 'big Ike' among them came to my house only a few days since when all were absent except my wife who is in bad health and was lying down at the time and as all the doors were closed he walked around to her bedroom window and stuck his head in with one of his cursed grunts and so frightened her that she has been since confined to her bed with doctor bills for me to foot up." In forwarding this trivial complaint to Agent Patten, the Commissioner of Indian Affairs severely demanded the use of "every exertion to keep the Utes on the reservation."[22]

The fact that the Utes were obliged to hunt off the reservation due to driving off of game by trespassing domestic herds occasioned a rash of unsubstantiated accusations: the Utes were wantonly killing off the game for the hides alone; they were maliciously setting fire to the countryside. The deputy postmaster of Pagosa Springs added "the well-known fact that they are purchasing great quantities of ammunition from some unscrupulous persons in this place and also whiskey." Agent Patten was flatly informed, "it is your duty to control them and rid us of the nuisance."[23]

Much more serious than these choleric outbursts were developments in the area of Ute Mountain and the adjacent Utah border. Some of the Wiminuches, Mariano, Red Jacket, and Narraguinup in particular, wintered their considerable horse herds in this area and clashed with quick-drawing cowboys in charge of large herds of cattle. To an extent these clashes resulted in depredations claims against the Government, in which lean range cattle were sometimes described as "pure dairy-bred cows" to justify high rates of compensation (see correspondence on Willis and Fleming case).[24]

A state of undeclared war developed with the employees of the British-owned Kansas and New Mexico Land and Cattle Company, whose large Colorado operations were managed by the Carlisle brothers. Neighboring homesteaders were often the victims of the hatreds engendered, and were quick to imagine widespread Indian plots. Early in 1882, an inspired rumor of an impending joint outbreak of Utes, Paiutes, and Navajos of Arizona, New Mexico, and Utah brought queries from Washington. It was alleged that the Mormons were furnishing the Indians with arms, ammunition, and whiskey to stimulate the uprising.[25] No doubt the commingling of Utes, Paiutes, and Navajos in the Four Corners area and their several claims to certain portions of the area lent substance to the imaginary intertribal plot. For instance, groups of homesteaders were apparently driven from what was at that time not clearly defined as Ute or Navajo land on McElmo Creek, and they apparently thought the Utes and Navajos had a united policy of exclusion.[26]

In 1884, a few of the Carlisle cowboys were killed in a clash with Indians. Ignacio denied that any Utes were involved, but Red Jacket was at that time rescuing from a military search party some Indians who had confessed to their part in the fracas.[27] The following June, a family of six sleeping Utes were murdered in their tent, and rumors spread that the Carlisle cowboys had thus taken their revenge. Commenting on this outrage in his Annual Report, Agent Stollsteimer said that the murderers were "unknown whites" and added, "even if they were known, I doubt whether the State authorities would take steps to arrest and punish them. An Indian is hardly considered a human being by a certain class of whites."[28] An anonymous informer told the Fort Lewis commander, Colonel Swaine, that Stollsteimer and the Utes knew exactly who the murderers were and that Stollsteimer intended to leave the Agency the following spring "before the grass is green," to avoid becoming involved in the retaliatory war planned by the Indians. As Swaine relayed the report to Stollsteimer, "The Indians are demanding that these men be captured and punished, but you are putting them off until you are out of office, as the community looks upon the murder of an Indian as just the thing and to prosecute these murderers would make you unpopular."

Another charge in the anonymous report was that Red Jacket, Mariano, Jim Hardy, and Senup, among others, stayed mostly with the Paiutes, going only occasionally to the Agency for rations and to lure away young "bucks" to join in their sprees of "killing cattle and stealing horses if not murder. . . . they are not missed by you, who issue rations to the chief offenders." These chiefs "have always talked war and have a party strong enough to overpower Ignacio's opposition."[29]

While the Utes at the western end of the reservation were trying to bar with threats and raids the land they considered theirs from entry by homesteaders and cowboys, Utes near the Agency were asking Stollsteimer to arrange for a delegation to Washington so that they could lay their grievances before the President. To this proposal, Indian Commissioner Upshaw replied: "You are advised that this office does not deem such a visit necessary at this time and you will so inform them."[30]

It was then that the Utes, sick unto death of sharpshooting cowboys, hostile and lawless ranchers, townsmen and horse thieves, and altogether disenchanted with life on their not-so-private reservation, listened to the counsel of tribesmen who proposed moving the reservation to the west. The genesis of this proposal is not altogether clear, but it was apparently the brainchild of those Wiminuches with large horse herds who ranged west of Ute Mountain, were in sharpest clash with the cowboys, and were the most adamant opponents to a transition to agriculture. Of these Utes, Stollsteimer said in 1887 that they had threatened to destroy the crops of the Kapotas and Muwaches who lived mainly at the east end of the reservation.[31]

Opinion among the Utes in favor of removal to the west was far from unanimous, but the Government was quick to respond to the proposal. Commissioner of Indian Affairs Atkins instructed Stollsteimer to select a delegation to come to Washington, admonishing him to bring two of the most influential Utes, making sure that they were proponents of removal.[32]

A delegation consisting of Ignacio, Buckskin Charley, and Tapuche, escorted by Stollsteimer and the interpreter, Colorado State Senator A. D. Archuleta, arrived in Washington in the early days of 1886. Consultation with Interior Department and Indian Office officials was followed by interviews with Congressional committees. In one recorded interview, Buckskin Charley served as spokesman, with the approval of Ignacio, who declared that what Charley said was "straight." Charley listed as the reasons why the Utes wished to exchange their present reservation for one in southeastern Utah the following:

1) The present reservation, being long and narrow, was open to constant intrusion and the Utes wanted a reservation of a shape that would guarantee some privacy.
2) According to Commission reports, they wanted to live nearer to their friends, the Navajos, and in an area of milder winters and better rangeland for their stock.
3) They did not want to be forced to send their children to boarding school ("when they go away, they die, and we cannot account for it") but would accept school facilities on the reservation.
4) They refused to consider removal to the Uintah reservation because there was not sufficient land for them to share with the Northern Utes.
5) They were tired of being invaded by the "border thief and desperado" element.
6) In southeastern Utah, with its limited water supply, they hoped for reduced contact with whites.

Charley also protested the withholding of cash payments the previous fall and the non-arrival of annuity goods, as well as of three large American stud horses previously promised. These items had been withheld apparently to break down Ute resistance to sending their children to boarding school after a disastrous experience at the Albuquerque Indian School in 1883-1885. Twelve out of the twenty-seven schoolchildren had died. In protest, Charley declared flatly, "these goods are not given to us for nothing, but come from the sale of our lands."[33]

From 1886 to 1895, the proposal for removal to southeastern Utah was discussed and negotiated in an atmosphere of growing controversy. Throughout, it became more and more debatable how many Utes actually wanted to move and for what reasons: a bigger share of open range for their stock, freedom from controversy with white settlers, and cattle interests, or surcease from Government pressure to become "civilized."

What is very clear is that factions grew among the Utes themselves over the issue of staying or going, that these factions were nurtured by outside interests seeking gain for themselves in one outcome or the other, and that Government intervention only acted to heighten the controversy. For one thing, passage of the Allotment Act of 1887 was used to place the issue in a new light: to remain on the old reservation under the condition of allotment in severalty or to move to Utah. Since most Utes feared severalty as a device that would reduce their collective strength and force an alien "civilization" upon them, many who had no desire to move were led to temporary support of the removal proposal. Another main source of confusion was the argumentative linking of allotment with gratuity payments and the attendance of children at boarding school.

A Southern Ute Commission, consisting of J. M. Smith, chairman, Thomas S. Childs, secretary, and R. B. Weaver, spent the latter half of 1888 negotiating with the Southern Utes. The Chairman's Report and the Secretary's Journal give ample evidence of the conflicting interests which confused the negotiations. For one thing, thirty-two leading men and their families had by now been settled on ranches on the Pine River south of the Agency, equipped with houses, fences, and irrigation ditches. Among them were Severo, Aguila, Tapuche, Juan Tobase, Shoshoni, Padre, Juan Juan Anche, Carneritch, Abiquiu, and Peketegone.

The only family actually farming these ranches was that of Aguila who, understandably, was the only Ute to declare in favor of allotment in severalty. The other thirty-one families did, however, benefit by renting their lands on shares to Spanish farmers. About 600 acres in all was under cultivation. The income from the ranches, added to rations, annuity supplies, and cash payments kept these families in comfortable circumstances.

Income was also derived by permitting "favored white men" to cut hay and pasture stock on the reservation, for a small consideration, apparently paid to leading Utes and not to the Utes in general. Prominently mentioned among the "favored" ones was ex-Indian Agent Christian Stollsteimer, whose considerable influence among the Utes was devoted to opposing removal. While still Agent, as a matter of fact, Stollsteimer had gone so far as to block approval of a survey of the western part of the reservation, according to the surveyor's accusation.[34]

The majority of the Utes, still living in shifting camps and partly dependent on hunting for subsistence, were found by the Commissioners in conditions described as deplorable. Between railroad and highway lines and the grazing herds of white stockmen, the reservation was so overrun that both game and feed for Indian ponies were depleted.

In the first councils held by the Commission, few espoused removal. Even the chiefs who had originally made the proposal in Washington now opposed it. In private, however, Blanco, Anavaricio, Ankatash, Philippi, Tapuche, and others declared that many Utes really did want removal.

A delegation of three from each band was selected to look over the proposed reservation lands in Utah. For the Kapotas, San Juan, Tapuche, and Talian's son Ohecha were selected; for the Wiminuches, Ignacio, Mariano, and Cabeza Blanca; for the Muwaches, Buckskin Charley, Ojo Blanco, and Aguila (now replaced by Charley as chief spokesman before the Government for the Muwaches). Aguila was opposed to the whole scheme; he declared that if the Utes moved he would nonetheless remain on his ranch, demanded pay for time taken off from farming, and made pointed references to unfulfilled Government obligations under the treaties. He insisted that Stollsteimer accompany the delegation.

Throughout the trip, according to Commission reports, the Utes were inclined to be "sulky" and to withdraw for private conferences in their own tongue. Whereas the Commission considered a reservation running from the Colorado-Utah line west to the Colorado River quite adequate, the Ute members of the party demanded an area from the Big Bend of the Dolores west to and including Moab; they saw no reason why the Mormon community there could not be removed for their benefit, just as they had been subjected to removal.

They cared not a fig for the "desert land entries" filed on their projected reservation by cattle interests, fourteen such entries having been filed directly or indirectly on behalf of their old enemies, the Carlisles. And, indeed, it appeared that these entries would not stand if the lands, as suspected, were not true desert. If the reservation limits were to be as proposed by the Commission, the Utes demanded additional compensation of 50,000 sheep and $100,000.

As the negotiations proceeded, Charley protested the Government demand that candidates for gratuity payments send their children away to school, which the Commissioners claimed was required by Article 6 of the 1868 Treaty. Charley said that "good conduct" was the sole criterion, and Commission Secretary Childs declared the contention valid, since many "deserving" Utes did not have children of school age. Ignacio, for instance, had lost his last child in the Albuquerque fiasco. Further dissatisfaction over gratuities arose from the inclusion of additional names on the list, which reduced the amounts of individual payments.

Late in 1888, the overwhelming majority of adult male Utes chose removal as an evil lesser than that of allotment. One hundred and eighty-two signatures were needed to submit the matter to Congress, but a total of 253 signatures was obtained, including those of 24 men who were off hunting but who were signed for by the chiefs. A bill for removal was passed by the Senate, February 25, 1889, and was passed on to the House Committee on Indian Affairs, where no further action was taken.[35]

In the years that followed, the issue of removal continued, with the drafting of new bills, the development of sharper lines of cleavage among the Utes, the constant intrusion of the school and gratuity questions into the controversy, and the active involvement of Southern Ute Agents as leaders of interest groups in Southwestern Colorado, supporting or opposing removal. Charles Bartholemew, Agent from 1889 to mid-1893, was an active leader of the removal forces and, while Agent, ran for elective office with the enthusiastic backing of those forces. In 1890, C. C. Painter of the Indian Rights Association was quoted in the press as having stated that two of the principal employees at the Southern Ute Agency had purchased farm machinery and stored it near the Agency, against that happy day when Ute removal would open the Pine River Valley to homesteaders.

Bartholemew penned a hot protest to Painter, who replied that he had been misquoted. What he had actually said was that the employees in question had stated "that they did not take their positions at the Southern Ute Agency for the salaries attached, but believing that the Indians would certainly be removed, they desired to be in a position to make selection of land." Painter further said that he had not publicly condemned such an attitude, but had stated that the Indians were surrounded by influences which were inimical to their remaining on their present reservation; only one employee was not outspokenly in favor of removal. Painter conceded that the Utes themselves were "almost unanimously in favor of going to Utah." He, however, had come to the conclusion that there would be "no civilization for the Indians in the removal."[36]

As part of the campaign for Ute removal, Bartholemew and his associates openly encouraged Ute opposition led by Ignacio to sending the children to off-reservation boarding schools. A month before the Fort Lewis school was scheduled to open in 1892, Commissioner of Indian Affairs Thomas Morgan instructed Bartholemew to try to collect 100 Ute children for the school, using such methods of compulsion as might seem "wise." He added severely that the Indian Office had frequently received information to the effect that Bartholemew was opposed to Ute attendance at the Fort Lewis school because he favored removal to Utah. Failure to fill the school with Ute children, therefore, would be construed as confirmation that Bartholemew was directing his efforts "to thwart the purpose of this office." Since Fort Lewis was so close to the reservation, Ute "repugnance" toward sending the children away to school should be at a minimum. It might also be wise to take the parents on a tour of inspection of the school to reassure them. [37]

Bartholemew made arrangements for the tour, but an outbreak of eye infections among the children already at Fort Lewis caused the Superintendent of Indian Schools to recommend a delay.[38] As a result, Ute resistance to the school was solidified and in mid-November Commissioner of Indian Affairs Morgan ordered the discharge of Ignacio as Captain of Indian Police, in retaliation for his leading role in the resistance. Henceforth, the Government would refuse to recognize him as the leading Ute. As for Bartholemew, Morgan said he had not "used proper means" to carry out instructions.[39]

The discharge of Ignacio was carried out under protest by Bartholemew, who stated that the old chief's influence for peace was universally recognized and that a "serious outbreak" was now to be feared.[40] All the leading citizens and businessmen of Durango, including such inveterate Ute-haters as D. L. Sheets, now sent a telegram to the Secretary of the Interior, protesting their undying love for Ignacio, denouncing the callous and even dangerous action of the Commissioner of Indian Affairs and demanding the return of Ignacio to his office.[41] Ignacio was forthwith restored as Chief of Police and Ute resistance to the Fort Lewis School continued as if nothing had happened. For a time, it appeared as if nothing could reverse the early prospect of Ute removal.

In 1893, however, an Executive Order directed that Army officers take over Indian agencies, in order to remove "local interests" from influence at the agencies. Bartholemew was removed from the helm at Southern Ute. At the same time, the overbearing Commissioner of Indian Affairs Morgan was replaced by D. M. Browning, who promptly rescinded orders for unlimited coercion of Indian parents to send their children to boarding schools. Although he authorized the withholding of rations or annuities in extreme cases, Browning upheld the recognition of parental rights, even those of "ignorant and superstitious parents."[42]

By now, the Utes had been subjected to years of uncertainty about their future and, at the same time, had gained some useful experience in dealing with officialdom at every level. Despite the heavy pressures exerted upon them, they had gained, rather than lost, confidence in their own ability to influence the outcome of issues. The bigoted Special Agent in charge of taking the 11th U.S. Census at Southern Ute in 1890 noted with annoyance that, "on account of the many recent interviews and conferences held with the Southern Utes by commissions and special agents regarding the proposed removal to Utah, these Indians now begin to think themselves very important and assume arrogant and self-important airs, their every action betraying a race of spoiled children. Their duplicity of character is well established."[43]

The Utes never lacked friends among other groups to whom they could turn when intercession was needed. These were most often Hispanic neighbors or people married into Hispanic families, like Timothy J. McClure of Durango. During the muddle over the Fort Lewis School and the downgrading of Ignacio, McClure was asked by Ignacio to write to Ute Commission Secretary Childs on his behalf. Reminding Childs of Ute patience in awaiting settlement of the removal question, McClure conveyed Ignacio's message that the Utes did not want to send their children to Fort Lewis but would welcome a school on their new reservation, "where they could be at home . . . they wanted the Great Father to understand that they were friendly and not mad."[44]

Late in 1893, the removal issue took a sharp tack, when the Army officer who briefly replaced Bartholemew as Agent was in turn replaced by David Day, the fiery editor of the *Durango Democrat*. He was an ardent advocate of allotment in severalty and so antagonized the removal advocates that they threatened to boycott his newspaper. His family was socially ostracized.[45]

The Imposition of Allotment

By 1894, Congress was reconsidering the wisdom of removal. From the House Committee on Indian Affairs came a recommendation for a return to the allotment provisions of the 1880 Agreement. It was recommended that a "diminished" section of the reservation at its western end be set aside for those Utes who were unalterably opposed to allotment.[46]

Agent Day insisted that many of the Utes did want to take up farming and were favorably disposed toward allotment, but that the Wiminuches, under the prodding of Ignacio and Mariano, were irreconcilable both to farming and to sending their children to the Fort Lewis School. As of October, 1894, the Wiminuches had ceased to come to the Agency, "other than when accompanying Durango citizens by rail." Day charged that the Durango businessmen were actively poisoning the minds of the Indians against allotment, and had paid off certain Ute chiefs to the tune of $10,000 to secure their continued resistance to allotment. As a result, "bad feeling" had been growing in the past ten years between the Wiminuches and the other bands.[47]

By the Act of February 20, 1895, Congress disapproved the Removal Agreement of 1888 and enacted the allotment provisions of the 1880 Agreement, to be carried out within six months. A diminished reservation was withheld for all Utes who refused or were not deemed qualified for allotment. All other unallotted lands east of the La Plata River were to be thrown open for sale to "bona fide" settlers at $1.25 per acre after allotment was completed.

Early in 1895, Meredith Kidd was appointed by the President as Commissioner to carry out the new allotment Act. Kidd was warned by Commissioner of Indian Affairs Browning, as he set out upon his task, to anticipate reluctance on the part of the Utes toward allotment, based on the following beliefs:

1) that the Government would arbitrarily take their lands without their consent;
2) that by accepting allotment they would lose the improvements made on lands they were now occupying;
3) that women and children would not be included in the per capita cash shares;
4) that, as they lost their present collective tenure, they would be "turned adrift and homeless,"
5) that those allotted at the east end of the reservation would have to travel to the west end for their annuities and rations, since the main Agency would be located there.

Browning urged maximum patience and explicit detail in explaining to the Utes how matters stood. He urged Kidd to make sure that the Indians received the cream of the agricultural land, and that they were permitted freely to select their own allotments.[48]

Meredith Kidd started his work at Southern Ute and the Allotting Commission was presently enlarged by the addition of David Day and a chairman from Texas, Julius Schutze. After prolonged negotiations, 375 Southern Utes accepted allotment; Francis Leupp of the Board of Indian Commissioners hailed this step as an achievement in "preventing the people of Colorado from driving the Southern Utes into Utah and putting upon them a reservation entirely unfitted for their advancement."

Meredith Kidd sharply dissented from this verdict. Having quarrelled ceaselessly with Agent Day during the long negotiations, he now charged that immediate allotment constituted a betrayal of long-term Ute interests: "They are wild, untamed savages, unfit for allotment, incapable of self-support. To remove the protecting arm of the Government and to throw them into the unequal struggle of competition with the whites, a struggle in which only the fittest would survive, would in my opinion be cruel and unjust."

To Kidd, the prospects for the unallotted Utes on the diminished reservation seemed brighter. For them, he advocated a program of obligatory instruction in industrious, sedentary farming life, with allotment as a goal only after they had become fully adjusted.[49] Kidd's opinion was barely noticed. For better or for worse, the issue of removal of the Southern Utes was permanently settled.

Chapter 3
Consequences of Allotment

The Land and Water Question

In 1895 two divergent systems of land tenure entered into operation among the Southern Utes. The allotted Ignacio Utes owned and inherited land as individuals and, with official permission, could lease their land. The unallotted Mountain Utes, on the other hand, shared land as collective property of the tribe. Portions could be leased with the consent of Ute Mountain leaders but could not be sold.

Since the purpose of allotment was to settle all the Ignacio Utes on farms of their own, the problem of water rights went hand-in-hand with the new form of land tenure. Agent Henry Page, as early as 1880, pointed out in his Annual Report that land on the Southern Ute reservation could not be cultivated without the use of irrigation ditches. The value of land in that area was and still is determined by access to water.

Individual ownership of land was foreign to the Utes and, for years following settlement on the reservation, they did not easily conceive of land as a commodity to be bought and sold. When they signed the 1874 Treaty, Agent Francis Weaver reported, they had thought that they were simply granting permission to gold rush prospectors to enter and establish mines and had not relinquished their rights to the area.[1]

Nonetheless, the Southern Utes became accustomed to ceding their claims to occupancy of large portions of their original range. Since they had been promised "perpetual" money payments and rations for as long as needed and since the game was already much reduced, the Utes accepted their losses with resignation.

The first experience of the Utes on their reservation in southwestern Colorado was one of confusion between land they considered theirs on the basis of past use and association and the boundaries defined by treaty. While the northern line at the foot of the mountains was understood when explained, the Utes were much more inclined to hold out for lands to the south and east where their old friends in the Indian Pueblos and Hispanic communities of New Mexico lived.

Weaver reported in a summary of his first months of work:

> Until my arrival here there was considerable harassing of the settlers north of
> the line of the Southern Ute reservation, but they now understand where the
> boundary is and have recognized it. But it seems impossible to get them to
> understand that their territory only extends south as far as the boundary of New
> Mexico and they lay claim to all the land south as far as the Cañon Largo and,
> as far as we can understand even further, in fact recognizing no Southern
> boundary at all. There are many white faces looking with covetous eyes upon
> this reservation, and from the greedy desire expressed to possess it, one would
> conclude that at no distant day it will by some result come under the control of
> the white man.[1]

Ute attachment to an area of range was different from the Anglo-American concept of property. In 1877, the band of the Wiminuch chief Cabezón was living along the La Plata River south of the reservation line. A number of Navajos lived with them, raising corn by the use of crude "sakas" (the Spanish word for irrigation ditch is "*acequia*"). In the winter of 1877-1878, Cabezón complained that, when the corn had been harvested in the fall of 1877 and the band had gone off on their fall hunt, two white settlers, Clayton and Roser, had moved in and filed a homestead claim on their land.

Cabezón said that Utes and Navajos had been living together on that spot since his boyhood and had there a site sacred to their annual corn feast. General Hatch of the Ute Commission was prepared to try to secure the plot permanently for Cabezón's band but, on second thought, Cabezón offered to move upstream on the La Plata after harvesting his 1878 crop.[2, 3]

The Utes accepted or rejected trespassers on their reservation according to the degree of inconvenience they caused and also according to their personal regard for particular trespassers. For instance, D. Culver of Animas City was summarily ordered to remove his sheep from the confluence of the Florida and Animas rivers in late 1877 because some Utes wanted to winter there.[4] That same fall, Ute leaders intervened to grant permission for Felipe Madrid of Tierra Amarilla to herd his 1,500 sheep on Ute Creek south of Lookout Knob, and no payment was mentioned.[5]

When Agent Weaver was forbidden by Ignacio to build a fence around the Agency dwellings and was only permitted to fence in the Agency garden patch as Ignacio instructed, the young Agent felt so indignant over this Ute arbitrariness that he penned an indignant letter to the Commissioner of Indian Affairs.[6] The record shows, however, that the Utes routinely objected for many years to fences as an impediment to the free movement of their grazing ponies.

As has been shown in the section on removal, the Utes early came to consider the cession of portions of their former range as a trade to be paid in cash and rations. They also developed a sufficiently astute business sense to start asking for payment *in advance* of a relinquishment and to demand extra cash payments for reduced acreage, as seen in the negotiations of 1888. They also became acquainted with the practice of accepting payment in cash or produce for the use of their land, as seen in the unofficial agreements on haycutting and grazing privileges made with favored friends and in the shares system practiced with Hispanic farmers from the mid-1880s. None of the above experiences, however, prepared the Utes for the change to individual land ownership under the Allotment Act, along with the additional complexities of tribal water rights, since in water adjudication the Government relied on the 1868 Treaty.

Within the FRC records, there is no forceful expression of Ute opinion on these land and water questions as problems until 1925. Possibly, this is due to the fact that they did not relate to land as a commodity nor to the concept of individual allotment.

The tracts allotted in 1895 consisted of 160 acres for the head of a family and 80 acres for each minor. Women living with their husbands were, in some cases but not generally, given separate allotments. Some chiefs received double allotments of 320 acres and orphaned minors were granted full allotments.

The total of allotted Utes in 1895 was 375, including some who at first refused allotment and asked to have their pre-allotment ranches sold but later relented. These were the headmen Ignacio, Tapuche, Nieves, and Juan Tobase. Commissioner of Indian Affairs Browning was so pleased with their decision that he directed they be granted 160 acres of improved land, plus an additional acreage of grazing land, and that their children, if they had not already done so, be given the opportunity of selecting allotments.[7]

David Day had the Utes select their improved lands along the river bottoms, starting with the Pine and proceeding to the Piedra and San Juan. Some few took up allotments along the Animas and La Plata. Along the Pine, the allotments were continuous to bar white neighbors, for fear of "bootleggers."[8]

If the allotted lands were to be cultivated, by Utes or others, irrigation ditches would have to be built. Some short, crude ditches had been built from the Pine River by Hispanic sharecroppers. The first survey and estimate for a ditch was projected in 1886[9] and in 1887 Agent Stollsteimer urged that irrigation work precede allotment in severalty.[10] In the meantime, however, non-Utes were taking water out of rivers to whose flow the Indians officially had first title under their treaties. Ditches had been built across reservation land with or without the permission of the government or the Indians.

An extreme example is provided by the La Plata Irrigating Ditch Company which, between 1889 and 1892, built a ditch across the Fort Lewis Military Reserve and the Southern Ute Reservation, followed by a request for right of way. It was refused, on the grounds that in a dry year the Fort Lewis School would be deprived of needed water. An appeal was rejected but in 1896 the company was still running La Plata water through its ditches, to the extent that the Utes farming the La Plata bottomlands had no irrigation water, according to Agent Day. Since the Fort Lewis Military Reserve was about to be restored to the public domain, Day urged that the Government file and record the entire La Plata flow for the Utes.[11]

As Allotment proceedings began, Day took note of the speed with which local homesteaders were filing and proving on water claims. He urged that Ute water rights be located and recorded before the "surplus" lands were opened for settlement, to "secure to the Utes water for all time to come." He was in particular haste to have a right of way for the Spring Creek Ditch, which he expected to start above the reservation line.[12]

Officialdom in Washington was less than concerned about the question of water rights for the Utes, apparently underestimating the effect of the Colorado water laws in an arid area where water was a primary concern. In Colorado, prior right was accorded to the party who first took water from a stream and then filed claim to its use by proving "beneficial use," beneficial, that is, to himself. Had the Government paid timely attention to the terms of Colorado water law, it could have forestalled the intricate and costly Pine River Water Adjudication.

In this suit, the prior right of the Utes to use of the Pine River flow, under the Treaty of 1868, had to be bolstered in court by evidence of some "beneficial use." As Acting U.S. Attorney Ernest Knaebel confided to the Attorney General early in the case in 1902, the issues to be settled were both difficult and urgent.[13]

The case was urgent because in a dry year the Pine River provided an inadequate flow to fill irrigation ditches, especially because it was drawn on by non-Utes upstream. Urgent, too, because as of 1896 Agent Day reported that many Pine River allotments were not reached by ditches.[14]

In 1908, numerous allotments were still not reached by ditches and, what made adjudication still more difficult, those Indians with water were not yet making full use of it, thus failing to meet the test of beneficial use. Assistant Engineer Blair Burwell urged, for this reason, that the Government build a reservoir to store the flood water of the Pine and give the Utes a "gilt-edged right" to its use.[15] It was many years before the Vallecito Reservoir was to become a reality. It was built with funds won by the Utes in their adjudication suit against the Government to compensate for deficient payment on relinquished lands.

Construction of the Vallecito Reservoir had dramatic consequences for the Southern Utes, foreseeable in view of what had gone before. Directly following Allotment, sales of allotted lands commenced, justified by the claim that elderly Utes who died had left no heirs. In the few instances where I was able to trace a Ute lineage, I became convinced that existing heirs were bypassed because they weren't present to make a claim.

Agency management knew full well that, upon the death of a member of the encampment, the family would place the body of the deceased, along with personal possessions, in a rock crevice. If the deceased was a warrior, his favorite horse would be slaughtered and its body added to the burial. The family would then leave the area for an extended period of time, much as bereaved Anglo-American families used to take a long trip following the death of a loved one. The Utes did not give notice of their departure and were treated as "deserters" for leaving their allotments. Agency management and Anglo-American neighbors seem to have been eager to have such lands placed in non-Ute hands, thereby depriving future generations of Utes of any rights whatever to land.

It must be noted, furthermore, that the Utes were never consulted about their concepts of kinship and heirship, nor did Agency personnel visit with Utes in their encampments and try to determine kin relationships among the camp members. Only one Agency farmer took the trouble to visit the camps and become acquainted with the residents of various camps.

The water rights that were supposed to be guaranteed to the Utes by the Vallecito Project passed to non-Utes along with the land sales. Even Reservation lands that had never been allotted to Utes acquired water rights when apportionment of water took place in the 1930s. The town of Allison, built on the site of the former Vallejos railroad construction camp at the south end of the Reservation, at first lacked irrigation water and, after a single spring hay crop, had to subsist on water from cisterns until water from the Vallecito transformed the community to the prosperous agricultural and livestock raising center it has become.

In view of the mounting complexities of land ownership and water rights and the squeezing of the Utes by land-hungry homesteaders and predatory corporations, the dark predictions of Meredith Kidd appeared likely to become reality. But this was not all. Allotment procedures, as previously described, led to inequalities, with headmen and their families receiving extra acreage. Besides, allotment to all children born as of 1895 without provision for those yet to be born led to greater inequalities.

High infant mortality left some bereaved parents with hundreds of acres inherited from their children while children born after allotment had to share their parents' 160 acres, of which only 80 were reckoned as irrigable. Small wonder, then, that by 1910 many such children had no land whatever. Meanwhile, some allotments had greatly increased in cash value while others were now rated as worthless.[16]

Some of the mushrooming problems brought on by the allotment procedures imposed upon reluctant and unready Utes were apparent as early as 1902. Terse answers by Agent Joseph Smith to a questionnaire from the Board of Indian Commissioners give the following information: There were still 375 allotments. All were still under 25-year restricted patents, that is, they could not be sold without the Government's permission. One hundred allottees were living at Navajo Springs with the unallotted Utes or on the allotments of relatives.

Eighty-eight allottees had died and, since no register of names and family relationships had been completed, identification of heirs was difficult. About half the allotments were judged to be sufficiently adaptable to agriculture so that an "industrious Indian" could support his family on 160 acres. Few Utes had yet become successful farmers, as attested by the fact that 964 allotted and unallotted Utes, practically all those in southwestern Colorado, were receiving rations. There had been no change for the past three years in the number of self-supporting Utes.[17]

Division of the allotments of deceased Utes among many heirs left some possessed of tiny tracts of virtually useless land. Coupled with that fact, even the most industrious Utes were as yet insufficiently adapted to farming to cultivate 80 acres. By 1910, a policy of selling inherited Indian lands was in full swing. Cash proceeds were divided equally among the heirs who then received reduced allotments of what was said to be choice land, heavily concentrated along the Pine River and Spring Creek valleys.

This policy was enthusiastically promoted by Superintendent Charles Werner, [18] mainly regarding sales of inherited lands). In his 1911 Annual Report, Werner proudly announced that in that year he had sold 1,040 acres of inherited land for $4,760 and 1,400 acres of "non-competent" land (meaning land in the hands of Indians who were judged non-competent to become farmers) for $11,213. The money from the sales had been deposited in Individual Indian Accounts and was available for the individual purchase of "surplus" Indian tracts in the Pine River Valley, as well as for equipment, furniture, and improvements.[19]

Werner advocated the policy of land sales in the name of Indian self-support. He predicted that intensive cultivation of small irrigated tracts plus the use of the proceeds of land sales would so benefit the Ignacio Utes that within a few years they would no longer need an Agency.[20] Yet the policy of reducing and concentrating Indian land holdings initiated by Werner and continued by his successors could not but militate against eventual self-support.

Holdings of forty acres or less were hardly adequate for an economy based on the raising of cattle and fodder crops. This was the economy of area non-Ute ranchers, which the Utes were being urged to emulate even while they were being deprived of the means of so doing. There is nothing in the FRC records, however, to indicate that the Utes were much perturbed at this time over the marked reduction of their land holdings. The inducement of ready cash was potent.

As ex-Agent David Day cynically observed to Assistant Commissioner of Indian Affairs Abbot in 1913: "Noticing that the Hon. Secretary is planning to render the Indians more of an asset than a liability, I might say nuisance, I am led to conclude that decreased land holdings, along the lines suggested, is not only to be commended but urged. . . . No Indian has use for more than forty acres. . . . If there is any one thing dear to a Ute Indian, it is a source of revenue."[21]

In late 1925 and early 1926, the Ignacio Utes suddenly reversed their attitude of apparent previous apathy toward their individual land holdings. Two rebellious and indignant delegations, the first of which was not officially recognized by the Government, swept into Washington. They presented a series of charges, first against their Superintendent, E. E. McKean, later including the entire Bureau of Indian Affairs.

The central point of these charges was a claim of mismanagement over many years and failure to account to the Utes for the spending of enormous sums of their money. These delegations and charges will be more fully described in a later section. What merits attention here was the charge laid against McKean that he had on "many occasions dislodged and dispossessed Southern Utes of their allotted lands by commanding them to sign deeds to their lands without their consent, and the Indians have been compelled to accept the amount handed to them by the Superintendent, which are generally not one fourth the value of the lands so sold."[22]

McKean denounced this charge as absolutely false, declaring that allotted lands were only sold upon the request and full consent of the allottees, also that many lands put up for sale remained unsold because they had been appraised at too high a figure.[23] Whatever the facts may be, the Ignacio Utes were now demonstrating a proprietary interest in their allotted lands. They were complaining, not alone of insufficient compensation for their lands, a matter which already aroused their indignation in 1877, but also of being arbitrarily pushed into selling their lands.

As a postscript to this section, it should be added that the dilemma of the proposed Animas-La Plata Project of the 1990s rests upon the long history of land misappropriation and water piracy on the Southern Utes reservation. Congress has approved funds ostensibly to satisfy Ute, Navajo, and Jicarilla Apache rights violated in the past. As described in the Afterword, the reality is one in which astronomical sums are being expended in a manner that will damage the environment while serving the interests of land developers and the mining industry. Had the concern for Indian water rights been genuine, the goals could have been accomplished at far lesser cost by buying out non-Indian landholdings sited on the Reservation, then restoring the water rights to Southern Ute ownership.

Administrators' Conflicting Interests

When the Ute delegations launched their charges against Superintendent McKean in 1925-1926, they accused him on many scores of representing the interests of Anglo-Americans to the Utes' disadvantage. This charge could as well have been made, although apparently it never came from Ute sources, against most of McKean's predecessors. Actually, in a region where Indian Affairs was from the outset a cornerstone of the local economy but where the Indians themselves were a disenfranchised minority of the local population, the Agent or Superintendent was subject to conflicting pressures and many temptations. The most compelling of these centered on land and water matters.

Henry Page, Agent from 1879 to 1881, was an unsuccessful candidate for elective office in Little Rock, Arkansas. He apparently received his post with the Southern Utes as a political consolation prize. He brought with him as his clerk a Little Rock freighter, Samuel Beaumont. Inspector Hayworth reported to the Indian Office that these two were often absent from the Agency for long periods, on personal business and to the detriment of Agency Affairs. The nature of the business was not spelled out.[24] It can be noted, however, that in his 1880 Annual Report, Page advocated emphasis on stockraising rather than agriculture, as being better suited to the climate as well as to the terrain of the reservation and to the propensities of the Utes.[25] Page also sent frequent inquiries to Washington regarding the prospects of Ute removal.

Since Henry Page apparently had no background to qualify him as an Indian Agent, perhaps his main interest in his post was the chance to file claim on Ute land in case removal was enacted. Moreover, although the pay for early Agents was scandalously low, the only Agent to resign his job on the grounds of insufficient pay was the first and most idealistic one, Francis Weaver.[26] Other

Agents, as Charles Bartholemew candidly stated, did not take the job for the pay but for other considerations.

The personal stake of Christian Stollsteimer, Agent from 1885 to 1887, in blocking plans for Ute removal has already been mentioned. By paying small amounts to Ute leaders, he enjoyed the use of reservation rangelands near his Piedra River ranch. A Land Office surveyor, sent in the spring of 1888 to examine and mark the northern boundary of the reservation west of Mesa Verde, accused Stollsteimer of failing to submit a certificate of approval for the survey, "for reasons of his own (apparent to me)." These reasons likely were Stollsteimer's known opposition to Ute removal.[27]

Charles Bartholemew, probably a member of an early family of ranchers on the Florida mesa, was an active spokesman for removal. In this, he apparently used Chief Ignacio as a cat's paw. It is significant that the U.S. Census agent of 1890 described Ignacio as ruling the Southern Utes "with an iron hand" but added that he was "perfectly subordinate to the Agent, obedient and tractable."[28]

David Day, Agent from late 1893 to 1897, fought for allotment and boasted of having achieved thereby "a degree of unpopularity in this vicinity that can only be duplicated by a 'sound money advocate,'" due to his "efforts in battling for law and justice as against prejudice and falsehood."[29] Day's later record, however, indicates that he had a possible long-range interest in allotment not motivated by simple considerations of justice for the Utes. Allotment was soon followed by progressive reduction of lands held by the Utes which then became subject to development by private interests. David Day was associated with one of these interests, the Eden Canal Land and Power Company. In 1909 and thereafter, this company sought a right of way for Animas River water in competition with the Citizens' Animas Ditch Company.[30]

The above instance is one illustration of the competition which developed between various private companies for the lucrative right to divert Indian water in ditches running across Indian lands to sell it to ranchers. In exchange for conceding rights of way, affected Utes were to have free or low-cost use of the minimal amount of water which they required. The Morrison Ditch is an example of this type of operation but the history of the Animas flow in the FRC records provides documentation of the involvement, not only of David Day but also of his brother-in-law, Agent Joseph Smith, during his tenure from 1900 to 1905.

In 1901, Smith proposed to the Indian Office a plan for the irrigation of nine Indian allotments along the Animas River, "through a proposed arrangement with certain white settlers." The first allotments belonged to María Antonia Head, her son and daughter by Carlos Tucsón, and her younger son by Juan José Vásquez, who applied on her behalf. María Antonia Head was supposedly a sister of the influential headman Severo. Having been raised in the home of Lafayette Head in the San Luis Valley, she had friends among hispanicized Utes who received allotments as her neighbors. By the proposed arrangement, the Government would first file for the water to perfect the Indians' title and would then carry the cost of building the ditch to the south line of the allotments. The settlers would bear the expense beyond that point and, in this way, the Indians would have water at "nominal cost."

The Indian Office found it inadvisable for Utes to share ownership of a ditch with settlers, predicting friction and complications. Injunction proceedings had been brought against Dr. S. W. Morrison for interference with the West Side ditch and the Office was awaiting judicial confirmation of the opinion of District Court Judge Hallett that Government-built Indian ditches were for a "public purpose" and therefore not subject to Colorado water law. Any ditch for the nine Ute allottees along the Animas must be built entirely at Government expense and for them only.[31]

The ditch for the Animas allottees was completed in 1905 but was almost immediately destroyed by rains and floods. The estimate for rebuilding it with proper protection was $5,000, which the Government refused to authorize. At this time, however, with the assistance of William Peterson, Superintendent of the Fort Lewis School, the ranchers of the Animas applied for and received Government permission to rebuild and enlarge the ditch, securing permanent rights to water in excess of 12 acre feet for the Indian allottees. The water was to be delivered free of charge to the allottees and their heirs.[32]

As it happened, ex-Agent Smith had a ranch on the Animas River near La Posta, handy to the head of the Animas ditch. He was a shareholder of the Ditch Company, whose secretary said of him: "Smith is the man who worked the original graft scheme on this ditch and was deposed as Indian Agent for incompetency."[33]

In light of his interests as a ranch owner with special advantages as Indian Agent, particular interest attaches to Smith's dismay upon learning that the western segment of the Southern Ute reservation was to be placed under the supervision of the Fort Lewis School superintendent. Smith said that he was delighted to be free of responsibility for the Navajo Springs Agency, serving nearly 600 Wiminuches, whom he described as "a hard lot to manage and very non-progressive." But he urged that the sub-Agency at Ignacio include all allotted Utes, specifying that the west bank of the Animas ought to be within his jurisdiction. In this way, he said, allotted parents would be kept on the same rolls as their children with allotments on different rivers.

Smith did not mention allotted Utes with lands on the La Plata, nor those living at Navajo Springs. Maybe he did not want another Indian Service employee to be in charge of the area where his ranch was located.[34, 35]

Whereas Indian allottees served by the Animas ditch received their water free, lessees of these allotments paid only half rate for water, a very advantageous arrangement.[36] The shareholders of the Ditch Company proposed to the Indian Office in 1913 that when 20 years of free water had passed, the Indians should start to pay. The Indian Office never approved this proposal. In 1925, the Ditch Company (now renamed the Citizens' Animas Irrigation Company) started billing the Ute allottees for water assessments, but were unable to collect. The Indian Office stated that the original agreement stood. Each allotment, whether owned by the original allottees or their heirs, was to receive 12 acre feet free of charge.

The entire matter came as a surprise both to the Utes and to their superintendent, E. E. McKean, although after eight years at Southern Ute he was well versed in local affairs. As for the Indian Office, checking the claims of the Company required extensive research. It is impressive that the records were actually found, since transactions of many years' standing were all too often lost in the files and the word of claimants was sometimes taken at face value.[37] When McKean notified the Utes that they need not pay, the Company retaliated by threatening to skip the Indians' ditches in their spring cleanup. It is hard to believe the Company secretary's allegation that the Animas ditch had "cost us three or four times what it would have to construct an independent ditch where we wanted it."[38]

Charles Werner, Superintendent at Ignacio from 1907 to mid-1912, became deeply involved in many local business transactions involving the land, water, and money of the Utes. By now, the Ignacio Superintendency must have acquired fame in the Indian Service as a happy hunting ground for employees. Both Werner and his predecessor, William Leonard, received offers to exchange posts from other superintendents, claiming to have heard of the "fine climate" of Ignacio. Since both superintendencies offered in exchange were larger and better established than the Ignacio Agency, it is interesting that neither Leonard nor Werner appear to have considered an exchange.[39]

Werner initiated the policy of selling inherited Indian lands and reducing many allotments to 40 acres. Werner's successor, Stephen Abbot, claimed that Werner had sold some of these lands below their true value and, while still Superintendent, had bought some of them himself.[40]

In 1909, Werner was involved in a series of charges and counter-charges with his financial clerk, Chester Smythe, whom he succeeded in ousting. According to Werner, Smythe had stirred up the Utes against himself and the trader, Hans Aspaas, by telling them that these two close friends were trying to "defraud them of their rights." Smythe had accused Werner of "aiding the men who opened the Carey Act lands." He was threatening to put Werner out of the Service "as he had Mr. Leonard two years ago." Werner's counter-charges were that Smythe was a confederate of ex-trader Roy Hall and that, in addition to repeated acts of insubordination, Smythe was hopelessly addicted to liquor to the point of bringing on delirium tremens.[41]

In the controversy over the Morrison ditch, Werner expressed himself as impartially favorable to granting permission to one or another of the contending claimants to carry Indian water to allotments west of the Pine River. He praised the offer of ditch space and right-of-way for the Indians' water as reasonable and less costly than the building of a new Indian ditch. No additional amount of water to the Indians need be considered in the agreement, since previous Indian filings for 349 feet of Pine River water were ample for their needs.[42]

A year later, the next regular Superintendent, Stephen Abbot, stated that private companies were claiming more water than the total flow of the Pine River. Through no fault of their own, the Utes were being penalized for their "backward state of civilization" in applying the law of "beneficial use."[43] Werner met the wishes of the Utes as well as of local businessmen by attempting to increase the roster of Indians declared competent to handle their own money, so that they could dispose of stated sums without explicit permission from Washington for each transaction.[44] In former years, businessmen had sold on credit, collecting their debts on Annuity Day, but in 1909 the Government ruled that its employees must not act as a collection agency. Creditors would have to take their own chances.

This ruling placed both the Indians and the businessmen in an awkward position. For instance, Bob Richards ran up a debt of $83.50 with Hans Aspaas, which Aspaas tried to collect after the 1909 ruling was published. Richards acknowledged the debt, was willing to pay, and had a bank balance which more than covered the amount[45] yet, apparently, the debt was never paid. In 1918, Aspaas was still trying to collect nearly $2,000 in old debts, including a large sum from Bob Richards.[46]

In 1910, the Government amended its ruling to permit payment of debts from Individual Indian Accounts if the purchases were necessary and the prices just and if the Indian debtor or his heirs were willing to pay.[47] This ruling, in effect, encouraged Indians to try to buy on credit and then to repudiate their debts.

The exertion of remote control by the Indian Office over Ute expenditures was sometimes galling in the extreme, due to disagreement on the definition of a "necessary" purchase. Utes, like many other Westerners, prized fine saddles.

Roy Watts, as a youth, was refused Washington authorization to invest $50 in a saddle, on the grounds that he would only be able to use it during school vacations and his father would get the main use of it.[48] Mary Baker Peña had to wait to complete the building of her family home until authorized to draw on her children's accounts. "I am writing to ask if you have had any permission from Washington yet about the money of my girls," wrote Mrs. Peña in some annoyance to Superintendent McKean. "[Y]ou don't write if you have had or not. It seems like you don't care if I have a house built or not just so you have your way."[49]

Judgments of Agents or Superintendents regarding the competence of Indians to handle their own money seem to have been correlated with degree of intimacy with the local businessmen and a desire to promote trade. Charles Bartholemew expressed complete confidence in the Utes' ability to manage their funds. Corroboration for his view came from the U.S. Census agent of 1890, who described the Ute method of keeping tally of their debts with the traders by cutting notches on a stick, each representing a dollar owed.[50]

In response to a query from the Commissioner of Indian Affairs dated 12/7/1892, regarding a proposal to commute Annuity clothing and rations to cash, Bartholemew replied that "there is no doubt as to the ability of the head of every family to make his purchases with his money as carefully and economically as the most frugal farmer or wage worker in the land. The Indian never buys what he don't want and his wants are simple. With money to buy he will purchase what he needs as far as his money goes no more no less . . . and the Indian will often travel 5 miles farther if he can secure an advantage in the investment of 50 cents."

Bartholemew said that, left to make their own decisions, the Indians would economize by buying low-grade local wheat and rough grade of beef with "lumpy jaw" and other defects. He held that cash payments would teach them self-support much better than the ration system, by which they were kept dependent, "always looking blindly to the Govt as a child will to its mother, and never giving the future a thought."[51]

It has been shown that Werner, whose relations with some local businessmen were as cordial as Bartholemew's, also found many Indians "competent." Captain Stephen Abbot, to the contrary, had a low opinion both of the local businessmen and of the Indians' competence. He wrote to the Commissioner: "It seems that during the last few years the public has been allowed to do exactly as they pleased on this reservation and perhaps on all the Indian allotments."[52] He hinted darkly that if the Commissioner could himself inspect irregularities in the conduct of Indian trading, the Trader's store would be closed. He accused Hans Aspaas, who had the contract for furnishing Indian beef, of being in collusion with José Velásquez, the Agency Additional Farmer, in providing animals of light weight and with such defects as lumpy jaw. This, wrote Abbot, offended the Indians. Having forced Velásquez to resign, Abbot personally inspected the beef.[53]

While convinced that he was acting in the interest of the Utes, Abbot stirred up so much resentment in the community that several episodes of shooting occurred at the Agency, one bullet landing in the bedroom of Miss Garton, the Matron. Angry Anglo, Hispanic, and Ute demonstrators threatened to kill a night watchman hired by Abbot to protect the Agency premises.[54]

In the handling of heirship cases, the Agent or Superintendent exerted control over the disposition of land and money. In these functions, he was under pressure both from the Indian Office, regarding procedures, and from elements in the community, regarding special interests. Before allotment, Annuity payments to minor orphans were generally made to whichever Utes were acting in loco parentis. These were usually either siblings, parents, or more remote relatives of the deceased parents.[55] As time passed, less attention was paid to recording relationships between the orphans and those who received the payments but, to the extent that I have been able to trace such relationships with Ute assistance, all the recipients were kin to the child. After allotment, however, legal guardians were appointed for minor orphans, most being non-Utes.

By 1899, the Indian Office was making pointed criticisms of the procedures by which guardians were appointed. The Commissioner of Indian Affairs wrote to Agent Louis Knackstedt that in many cases administrators of estates and guardians of minors proved to be irresponsible parties without adequate sureties. As citizens, the allotted Utes were entitled to protection by the County or Probate courts of the State of Colorado in matters of heirship and wardship. The Agent should propose to the County or Probate judges "proper and fit persons . . . whether Indian or white," to serve as administrators or guardians. Such persons should be investigated for fitness and no payments should be made to minor wards until satisfactory guardianship was established.[56]

When Charles Werner was Superintendent, he had himself appointed guardian for a number of minors. His bondsmen were local businessmen whose listed assets covered the value of the estates. A later Superintendent, Walter Runke, objected to such arrangements on the grounds that they would place him under obligation to members of the community in the transaction of his official duties. He proposed that the Government directly convey the interests of minors, since appointed guardians were not, in fact, in charge of estates. To this, the Commissioner of Indian Affairs replied that, under Colorado law, only a court-appointed legal guardian could execute valid deeds on behalf of minors. The Secretary of the Interior could only approve or disapprove of such deeds.[57]

The Probate Judge of La Plata County, Richard McCloud, in a letter regarding one of the guardians, explained to Superintendent McKean: "The object for the appointment was to sell real estate."[58] This candid statement of a more than academic local interest highlights why many neighbors of the Utes cared who served as guardians as they sought to obtain Indian lands. For some years sale of such lands was expedited with the help of guardians who were often Agency employees.

Another link between the Agency and the Anglo community was forged by the licensed Indian Traders. At times they formed close friendships with Agency personnel and at other times feuds developed. In some instances, relations appear to have been somewhat irregular. When Ed Schiffer lost his Trader's license in 1886, he fought back by notifying the Indian Office that Agent Stollsteimer was circulating the rumor that he could have his license renewed by offering a $500 bribe to someone in the Office. In a letter from the Office, Stollsteimer was sharply questioned as to his guilt of "such a gross dereliction of duty."[59]

Traders enjoyed a protected position and felt free to complain to the Agent if the Utes bought at outside stores.[60] Joseph Smith, while Agent, became part-owner with a trader of a herd of cattle. This fact alone was considered sufficient to justify his removal.[61] Charles Werner's friendship with Hans Aspaas likewise may have contributed to his politically maneuvered dismissal, as well as to the loss of the Trader's post by Aspaas. A year later, Captain Abbot devoted much of his energy as Superintendent to pursuing a feud with Aspaas which even extended to Aspaas's employee, Tomás García, whom he hauled before a Justice of the Peace for taking two cast-iron pipes from the Agency Condemned Heap. This was Abbot's idea of an object lesson on the sanctity of Government property.[62]

The trend in Agency affairs to grant special favors to non-Utes was fueled by frequent changes in leading personnel, namely, Agents-Superintendents and clerks. Records of Ute ownership and heirship frequently became confused and, as the Indians could not monitor the Agency, matters could be handled as the individual Superintendent saw fit.[63] Since no Agency leader ever expressed feelings of empathy for the Utes while most had friendships with at least some Anglos in the community, it is little wonder that many of them were denounced for collusion to defraud the Utes by inspectors or later Superintendents.

Trends toward accommodation of the Anglo community actually inhibited the very changes in Ute ways advocated in the Schurz program. The long drawn out issue of removal slowed down the program for farming, education, and settled abode. Until 1895, requests for authority to build or to set up training programs were frequently deferred pending settlement of the Ute removal question. For instance, the day-school building erected in 1886, with a dormitory added later, became unusable in 1890. The school was simply closed and no Indian Service school existed at the Ignacio Agency until 1902.

The same sort of thing happened when the first irrigation ditches became clogged or when the hiring of Agency farmers was requested. By the time that allotment was suddenly enacted, no advance preparations had been made for the momentous transition to a settled life on individually owned farms.

The Ignacio Utes were forthwith expected to behave like industrious farming citizens on their unprepared agricultural tracts, each with grazing land that in most instances was inadequate for running stock. Each family nominally owned funds that were closely guarded from their use in the Treasury or in Individual Indian Accounts. In effect, the Utes were being ordered, like Joseph's people in Egypt, to make bricks without straw.[64]

During the years 1877-1895, the Utes lived as best they could, some much better than others but most hunting for part of their larder. By a clause in the Brunot Agreement of 1874, confirmed in the Act of 1880, the Utes had a right to hunt on their ceded lands so long as there was game and a state of peace with the white population. Due to lack of game on the reservation, the Utes continued to make use of this right, despite constant protests and threats by white settlers, many of them unaware of the treaty rights of the Indians. Off-reservation hunting became increasingly dangerous after the 1889 statement of the Commissioner of Indian Affairs that the Government could not take responsibility for the safety of Indians off reservation, "in view of the known hostility of a lawless class of white people in Colorado and their desire to create disturbance and trouble."[65]

Hunting trips, visits to relatives in Utah, and expense-paid participation in Wild West shows[66] occupied much of the time of the Southern Utes during the years before and immediately after allotment, easing some of their economic problems. These activities, however, also kept them off the reservation and removed from the influences for directed culture change which were supposedly operative there.

It seems likely, therefore, that much of the marked change in Ute ways observable by the early 1900s was due more to informal intercultural contact than to effective operation of the Government program.

Chapter 4
Crisis: "Self-Support"

The Utes had been promised food rations for as long as they needed them, as well as annuities in goods and cash in perpetuity, by the Treaty of 1868 and Brunot Agreement of 1874. In Section 3 of the Act of 3/5/1875, however, Congress stipulated that Indians receiving rations must perform labor. When this stipulation was laid before the Utes, their reaction was explosive. Early in 1878, Agent Weaver reported despairingly to the Commissioner of Indian Affairs that he had discussed the matter in council with the Wiminuches plus the few Kapotas present, and that the collective response had been the same as that in private discussions:

> There are no words sufficiently expressive to represent the indolence of these Utes. They will do nothing except it can be done from the back of a horse. They regard all labor as degrading. When asked what they are to do for a livelihood now that the game is disappearing, they reply that their fathers lived by the chase and they will wait until all the game is gone, and then the Great Father will supply them abundantly in consideration of the land they sold him "treaty of '72" and further that they have already paid for what they are receiving now and in the future and that they cannot work. The chiefs further say that they were told at Washington that their hands were too soft and would not be expected to work. In this connection the agent cannot but express his disappointment and humiliation in failing in his undertaking the prime object of which was to teach these Utes work and finally to lift them up higher. This in my opinion cannot be done without a force sufficient to compel them to labor, taking away from them their horses and breaking up the nomadic mania, which is constitutional in these bands. If accomplished otherwise it must be the result of many years of patient effort.[1]

The Commissioner of Indian Affairs replied that the Utes could be exempted from the requirement to work for rations until "there is a force of employees to instruct them and implements are provided."[2] Neither then nor later did the Indian Office appear to take notice of the fact that its plans envisaged not only sweeping change in Ute means of subsistence but also the imposition upon Ute men of tasks they considered more appropriate for women and children. Weaver had noted that the Ute women, assisted by children, cared for the livestock and performed all the menial tasks; yet no program for teaching women to farm was at any time considered. Among those who received farm implements in the pre-allotment days, only a few widows were included.[3]

The Indian Office proposed to start the Utes on the road to self-support by furnishing them with stock cattle, sheep, and horses, and with agricultural implements, estimating an expenditure of $17 per man, woman, and child. This was to be financed from accumulated interest from the Ute 5% Fund, money set aside under the Brunot Agreement of 1874.[4] Weaver, however, declined to set up an estimate for this purpose, since the Utes had just voted their preference for an Indian Office under the military. Their aim was to duck being forced to farm and, if the Agency were moved to the Navajo River, farming would be precluded:

> As to horses, they have already too many, and horned cattle they would I have reason to believe slaughter. In case the animals estimated for is purchased for them, they should be given so many to each individual. If given to the head of the family, for the family and he or she should die the entire number would be killed and burned. Of the few families who have some sheep or goats, one of the possessors of the latter died yesterday morning when fifty goats, all which the family possessed being in the name of the deceased, all were slaughtered . . . . and with regard to the estimate for Merino Rams, it is exceedingly doubtful whether these should be purchased unless they can be taught to shear their sheep which they will not do now. . . . and in case they are to be compelled to learn to farm here, it will be necessary first to take out the necessary ditches for irrigation.[5]

No further efforts were made for several years to start the Utes farming and stockraising. Henry Page secured exemption for all able-bodied male Utes "until further notice" from labor equivalent to the value of rations received.[6] In 1883, however, the Government purchased 5,000 sheep at $2.70 per head for distribution among the Utes. The *Durango Herald* promptly charged that the "worthless cumberers of the choicest lands in La Plata County" were selling them to "Mexicans" at 50-75¢ per head. The Secretary of the Interior inquired about this "abuse," informing Agent Warren Patten that the Utes could not legally sell sheep provided by the Government; any sheep they sold must be returned. Patten replied that in reality few such sales had occurred.[7]

That winter, the Utes slaughtered their sheep in great numbers, because they found the beef ration insufficient. The estimate for beef per person per day amounted roughly to one pound gross, including hides, bones, and hooves. Since this estimate included infants in arms and since the Utes wasted little, consuming what to others was offal, it is hard to understand why they were so hard up for meat if, indeed, they were receiving their full beef ration.[8]

One reason for shortages in beef was no doubt the dwindling of weight and numbers between ration days due to lack of feed. The Agency employees were supposed to cut and cure hay in sufficient quantity to feed the stock through the winter, but were deterred by Ute objections to fenced pastures. What little hay was raised was lost in drought years, necessitating frequent emergency purchases of Open Market feed.[9]

In slow, piecemeal fashion, in the midst of a growing outlook for Ute removal to Utah, some attempts to initiate farming were undertaken. In 1884, construction of an irrigation ditch 1.5 miles long, clearing of 160 acres of land and purchase of fence posts, wire, staples, plows, and seed were authorized.[10] In 1887, the expenditure of $2,560 was authorized to build 10 miles of irrigation ditches on the reservation, "so that Indian farms may be opened and the Utes encouraged to engage in Agricultural pursuits."[11]

These expenditures led to the shares agreements between individual Utes and Hispanic farmers. Thirty-one out of 32 Ute families were supposedly engaged in farming in 1888, resulting in some prosperity for these families. These were the families to whom issues of farm implements and seeds were made in the pre-allotment years, as "industrious and deserving Indians"[12] and the same names also appear on the rolls of proposed Gratuity lists as "Indians who have distinguished themselves by good sense, energy and perseverance in the pursuits of civilized life and in the promotion of a good understanding between the Indians and the Government and people of the United States."[13]

The first Gratuity payment of 1881 was limited to seven chiefs and sub-chiefs but subsequent payrolls through the ten years of Gratuity payments show a spread of distribution to up to 34 people, going far beyond the principal headmen; in fact, all people of influence, from shamans to people with farms were included in the 1890 Gratuity Roll.[14]

Through the pre-allotment years, about half the names on the Gratuity Rolls are also found in the listing of Indian Police. While the pay was nominal, it constituted a steady monthly cash income.[15]

In the course of years of preferential treatment, therefore, a small percentage of Utes actually became nominally self-supporting. The experience of subsequent years was to show, however, that a firm basis for continued self-support had not been laid. Among the most enterprising and farm-oriented leaders interviewed by the Southern Ute Commission in 1888, Severo and Buckskin Charley still expressed confidence that Government rations would always be forthcoming as previously promised, and that general "good conduct" rather than more exacting requirements should be the condition for continuing Government support.[16]

During the early years, Utes were hired as temporary laborers when irrigation lines were being built, but few Utes other than the Police were ever on steady wages. James Allen (Phillipi) was hired as an Irregular Herder during the 1880s, being once dismissed for neglect of his duties. The Agency Interpreter for many years was John Taylor, an African American Army veteran married to a Ute. Job Cooper (Luis Ortiz), a Taos Indian who married a Ute woman and remained long enough to receive Allotment Number 54, was for some time a Blacksmith's Apprentice.[12] Until after 1900, this was the total of Utes or spouses of Utes employed by the Agency other than as Indian Police for more than brief periods.[17]

Directives from Washington from time to time urged the hiring of Indians. Agent Stollsteimer was instructed: "as it is the policy of this Office to employ Indians in every position they are competent to fill, such as teamsters, laborers, herders, etc., you will govern yourself accordingly."[18] Agent McCunniff was told to seek Indian employees for the school in Fiscal 1890, especially assistant cooks, assistant laundresses, and assistant seamstresses. He was also told to employ Indians who were competent and willing in positions other than those listed for Indians.[19]

Such instructions resulted in no increased hiring of Utes and, in view of the continued "nomadic mania," this is hardly surprising. In 1893, the Utes were still in shifting residence, occupying tepees and brush shelters, although the Government had built ten frame houses for the chiefs and fifteen families had built wattle-and-daub houses. These houses were used for storage rather than for residence. Especially the Wiminuches, living on the western half of the reservation, divided their time between hunting and stock raising, and kept on the move. The Agent, Major Freeman, reported in 1893 that three-fourths of the total of 4,000 horses, 50 cattle, 3,000 sheep, and 1,000 goats owned by Utes were in Wiminuch hands, but he did not describe how they were distributed. The removal question was then at a peak, and Major Freeman said that while the Utes seemed ready for rapid advance they had hitherto received so little encouragement and were now in such a state of uncertainty that he saw no immediate prospects of progress.[20]

Photo 4.1. Kitty Cloud and Euterpe (Terpe) Taylor
Kitty Cloud was John Taylor's wife and Euterpe Taylor was his daughter.
(Frances Leon Quintana, with permission)

Photo 4.2. Sam Taylor
(J. E. Candelaria Collection, with permission)

Once secure in the receipt of food rations, annuity goods, and cash, and with some added resources from the tenant-operated ranches, the Utes appeared less frequently at Anglo ranches in quest of a meal. This was a practice bitterly resented by the ranchers, who considered it a form of blackmail directed especially against their womenfolk. To the Utes, feeding visiting strangers apparently fell within their own practice of hospitality. Reporting on some McElmo ranchers' complaints of frequent Ute demands on their wives to cook them a meal, L. M. Armstrong observed philosophically to Agent Stollsteimer: "Well, I see nothing for the people to scare at, only the Utes seem hungry and make a bluff to get something to eat."[21]

Over the years, so little real offense or threat was offered by the Utes against their neighbors that Major Freeman remarked in his 1893 Annual Report that white women thought nothing of driving alone clear across the reservation. The repeated requests by early settlers for armed protection by "our boys in blue," lest their women be left "at the red devil's mercy" were, in the main, exaggerated expressions of annoyance rather than of fear.[20]

Government policy in the drive to settle the Utes on farms suffered some inconsistencies. These were apparent from the start. In 1884, Agent William Clark received authority to spend $1,600 "for such Indians as were anxious to engage in farming." There being only four such, he was able to give them a lavish start. The following year, Agent Stollsteimer submitted an estimate of $352.50 for seed to start eight more Indian families on farms, but was turned down cold, with expressions of disapproval over his extravagance.[22]

Pressure was strong on Agency employees to show some results. Stollsteimer was told by the Commissioner of Indian Affairs in 1886 that his qualifications as Agent and the merit of all his employees would be judged by their success in enlarging the acreage tilled by the Utes that year, and in requiring labor in exchange for rations. All Agency employees were to go out on the reservation and show the Utes "by personal example that you do not consider it degrading to honestly labor with your own hands for independence."[23]

On the other hand, deficiencies in Agency personnel and equipment were perennial. When there was a Farmer-in-Charge at the Agency, he was often a man without experience in southwestern irrigation methods. The hiring of Hispanic farmers, who were well versed in irrigation methods and best able to communicate with the Utes, was not favored. Furthermore, Government penny-pinching and emphasis on hand labor kept the techniques employed in Indian farming for some years behind the practices of the local Anglo ranchers.

In 1884, Agent Patten's request for authority to make an Open Market purchase of a reaper was denied on the grounds that the Secretary of the Interior "refuses to sanction the purchase of labor-saving machinery at Indian Agencies."[24] Superintendent Leonard was refused authority to purchase two sulky (small riding) plows and two gang (double riding) plows for the Indians on the grounds that the hand plow was considered "sufficient for their use."[25]

Between 1908 and 1912, Superintendent Werner put in repeated requests for authority to spend money on modern farm equipment, choice stock, and ditch repair, with little success. His efforts to replace an Acme harvester with a heavier and more expensive one produced by McCormick were long debated. Werner contended that the Acme was an expensive economy, since it frequently broke down on the heavy clay soil, corrugated for irrigation. During repairs, McCormicks had to be hired and, meanwhile, the Indians became discouraged over their unharvested crops standing in the fields.[26]

Sometimes, an impatient Ute moved ahead on his own to solve farming problems. In the early 1900s, to induce the Indians to farm, the Agency Farmer went out with a binder to harvest the Ute grain. In 1906, while the Agency binder was out of order, Severo bought one for himself, to make sure he got his crop in, and the Agency then rented Severo's binder.[27]

Despite all the factors making for halting and uneven progress of the Utes toward a farming economy, they were at no time totally dependent on rations, which by 1900 were considerably reduced. In his Annual Report for that year, the Commissioner of Indian Affairs announced that as against an estimated annual cost for full rations of $51, and an average expense for all tribes of $35 per person, rations for the Utes of Southwestern Colorado, averaged among 972 people, were only $13 per person.[28] Southern Utes of the 1960s who remembered back to those days also remembered keenly how they suffered from increasingly chronic hunger.

In 1900, the Government tried to propel the Utes toward a new advance in self-support. Distribution of Government seed for planting was refused on the grounds that the Utes had been instructed to save seed from the previous year's harvest. Agent Joseph Smith begged a year's stay on this order, promising to have the men in charge of the threshing machine at harvest time collect seed from the Utes for planting in 1901. Darkly describing the "absolute idleness of the allotted Utes," he predicted that unless seed was granted in the year 1900, the Utes would retaliate by refusing to work. "The fine farms along the big ditches on the reservation will lie idle" and no new ranches would be opened.[29]

Apparently, the seed requested was issued after all, for in September a fine crop was announced, with predictions for good market prices on the produce raised by the Utes. Ditches were being built from the San Juan and Piedra rivers, and relatives visiting the Utes at the Agency had "enjoyed the pleasant surroundings of our agency."[30]

From 1900 on, the Government increasingly emphasized work programs with reduced outlay of Indian funds. Here was foreshadowed the "Reimbursable" program, formally launched on the heels of the Ute Claims Decision in 1911. Under this program, individual Indians received advances out of the Reimbursable Fund, moneys set aside from the Judgment Fund, and repaid the advances in cash, kind, or labor. In the years prior to the formal establishment of the fund, repayment in kind or in labor was the principal objective promoted.

The Utes from first to last resisted this objective, never surrendering their original position that the Government owed them money and a livelihood under the treaties. In 1891, it was proposed that Indians receiving rations should be required to perform a certain number of days' labor on reservation roads and bridges, as an effective substitute for the taxes required of citizens.[31] Nothing came of it.

In 1903, when Agent Smith requested authority to spend $500 for labor to clean and repair the irrigation ditches, he was brusquely refused: "It is the policy of the Office to require the Indians to rely upon their own resources as far as possible, and as the Government has constructed a series of irrigation ditches, they can make a living if they will only keep the ditches in repair and in proper condition." If the Agent could not get the Indians to repair their own ditches, "it would seem that they are not worthy of further assistance."[32]

In 1908, Superintendent Werner was instructed to explain to the Utes the policy of requiring labor or equivalent repayment for tools received:

> The purpose of the law and regulations, as you doubtless appreciate, is to root out as rapidly as circumstances will justify it, the notion that at one time obtained so firm a hold upon the minds of Indians everywhere that the function of the Government was the distribution of gratuities. The pauperizing influence of this idea has been insidious, but far reaching, and will continue to do its damage wherever the greatest care is not taken in making the Indian understand that he must give an honest quid pro quo for everything he receives from the Government's hands.[33]

As has previously been stated, Superintendent Werner in 1912 strongly advocated a policy which he had been actively pursuing for several years, that of concentrating the allotted Utes on reduced acreages in the Pine River and Spring Creek valleys. "Surplus" lands were sold and with the proceeds Werner claimed that the Utes could advance within the next ten years to a status of self-support which would render Agency administration unnecessary "beyond someone to guard their interests."[34]

Contrary to the above rosy forecast, William Fry, who briefly served as Supervisor at the Agency in the fall of 1912, saw further obstacles to the successful practice of farming among the Utes:

> An enormous acreage (comparatively) for which water is available is not being used by the Indians for the reason advanced by some that seed is not available, by others that the agricultural implements necessary are not there, that after they get their crops in and are ready for harvesting the machines are not available for doing it, and a number of other reasons. They do not, of course, advance one of the real reasons, and that is a lack of application and industry on their part. If instead of loafing in town and the agency, the Indians would put in a reasonable number of hours each day in the cultivation of their land, there is no telling to what extent their crops will reach.[35]

Fry pointed out how well Anglo and "Mexican" farmers were doing on lands adjacent to the allotments. In late 1912 he had tried to persuade the Indians to extend their cultivated lands, by demonstrating "how anxious the Mexicans were to come in and use the Indians' farms and equipment on shares. This sort of business the Indians like, as it enables them to get a fair (?) remuneration without any labor on their part." Fry was in favor of shares agreements, so long as the Indians would divide the work with the Hispanos, but not as an excuse for them to loaf. Likewise, he advocated prompt delivery of seeds, implements, and a thresher, but purchased with the Utes' own funds.

Fry expressed approval of shares agreements for the running of cattle between the Agency Additional Farmer, José Velásquez, and five Utes, although regulations forbade business agreements between Indian Service employees and their charges. Under these agreements, the individuals who took over the care of Velásquez's cows were supposed to return double the number at the end of five years, and keep the rest. The agreements had been made with the knowledge of Superintendent Werner before Velásquez was aware that they were irregular. Said Fry: "and it appears to me that the Indians are getting the big end of the deal, and for that reason, if the transactions are not in actual conflict with Circular 318 and other Office regulations," the agreements should not be abrogated, but neither should they be renewed when terminated.[36]

Velásquez, when brought up on charges for these and other transactions, protested that his terms were better than those normally offered for local shares agreements, and that he had "desired to help these Indians and I knew that I could look after them and teach them how to care for the cattle and they could benefit by them." Velásquez took his cattle back from the Indians as instructed, paid them off, and made a new shares agreement with an Anglo.[37]

The irascible Captain Stephen Abbot, arriving upon the scene as Superintendent early in 1913, came to speedy, negative conclusions regarding the relations of Velásquez with the Utes: "Because I am convinced that ninety-five per cent of white farmers will do more than twice as much work as any Mexican I have ever seen, I told Velásquez I would accept his resignation. . . . I do not believe a Mexican is capable of teaching the Indian. The average Mexican is too much like the Indian."[38] Velásquez duly resigned, but then protested to the Indian Office that his resignation had been forced. Abbot retaliated by accusing Velásquez of entering partnership with the noted bootlegger Fabián Martínez shortly after leaving the Agency. The charge was refuted, but Velásquez did not return to Agency employ.[39]

The FRC records contain no direct proof of "uplift" or hurt to the Utes through shares agreements. It is clear, however, that the agreements were voluntary and also stimulated the Utes to participate in a form of locally recognized economic activity, common among both the Hispanos and many Anglos of the area. The abrogation of such agreements through Government intervention could only reduce participation, slowing down progress toward self-support, no matter how sincere the intention to protect "the best interests of the Utes."

By a 1910 court decision, the Utes suddenly seemed to be on the way to winning some of the riches that had been promised them when they relinquished their lands. A claims suit initiated in 1896 with the enthusiastic participation of the allotted Southern Utes[40] led to a judgment in favor of the Confederated Bands of Utes which in 1911 was found to amount to $3,305,257.19 for U.S. Government indebtedness on lands ceded in 1880.[41] The total share of the Southern Utes, including proceeds from lands sold after allotment, was $773,409.36. A Congressional appropriation in 1913 allowed $100,000 to all the Ute Bands, chargeable against the Judgment Fund. The Southern Ute share was $35,850.63.[42]

The Indian Office proceeded to institute plans for the utilization of the Utes' new wealth. Charles L. Davis was sent as Supervisor of Farming to study and report on economic conditions at all three Ute jurisdictions, and to recommend new measures. Davis reported that, of the 375 original Ignacio Ute allotments, with an acreage of 36,000 agricultural, 30,000 grazing, and 65,000 timberland acres, 103 allotments, totaling 16,340 acres, had been sold. Since the restricted patents would expire in 1921, leaving the Utes free to sell their lands at will, time was running short to prepare them for the transition. Davis wrote: "As a matter of fact the Indians have been left very largely to their own devises and about nothing has been done to aid or encourage them to extend their efforts in agricultural pursuits. The wonder is they have done so well as they have." Davis gave figures on acreage cultivated, crops raised, and stock owned by Utes, which leaned heavily on ex-Superintendent Werner's 1912 Annual Report. These figures shortly thereafter were so sharply challenged by Agency Farmer S. K. Emerson that they will be discussed in a later section.

Davis criticized the employment of the Agency Expert Farmer at the school, the use of the Additional Farmer as stableman, and the neglect of Indians farming on the reservation.[43] He and Superintendent Abbot had agreed on a plan for dividing the reservation into three districts, each under the supervision of a farmer with time and transportation facilities to visit the Indian farms.

Davis listed as the three practices most tending to "debauch" the Indians:

1) The issue of tools and implements without payment in money or labor.
2) The hiring of Utes (or, more often, Navajos) to clean the Indian ditches each year. The Utes were led to expect such things to be done for them, and to receive rations in addition.
3) The issue of seed without arrangements to return it or to pay for it after the harvest.

Davis and Abbot agreed on the desirability of limiting rations for able-bodied men to a "working ration" for those who were needy while working their farms. In preceding years, the $30,000 subsistence fund, guaranteed annually for distribution among the bands by the Treaty of 1868, had been increasingly limited to old, sick, or disabled Indians. Many of the dependents of able-bodied Ute men in Ignacio, however, were receiving rations. In Fiscal Year 1913, the total receiving rations at Ignacio numbered 178, out of a total population of 367, at a cost of $24.84 per individual, adding up to $4,422.85.

Davis argued that the subsistence fund as used was often a reward for indolence. He also proposed that in the new "working ration" bacon and beans be substituted for the traditional beef. He further proposed that the terms regulating the subsistence fund be amended to permit diversion of money from the specified foods to seed, implements, etc., whose increase would reduce the need for rations; this would aid industry "instead of feeding them in idleness." This recommended change in the terms of the $30,000 appropriation was rejected by the Commissioner, with the understanding that it would be borne in mind when the F.Y. 1915 Annual Estimate was prepared.[44]

Davis took issue with the decision by Congress to use the interest on the Judgment Fund to make annual per capita payments to the Utes of all jurisdictions, which he estimated would amount to about $64 per individual. He noted that for many years past annual spring per capita payments, averaging $18 per person, were fast spent on subsistence and clothing, often going directly to the Trader to cover past debts.

Davis considered these small payments "more injurious than helpful," since they relieved immediate wants without ever providing the possibility of "industrial uplift and welfare." He proposed for Fiscal Year 1914 a $20 per capita payment merely as a concession to habit. In the future Congress should make available $1,000,000 from the principal of the Judgment Fund for the "permanent benefit of the Indians." This would make available about $480 apiece for approximately 2,045 Utes, of whom 1,185, more than half, were Northern Utes. The money should be deposited in Individual Indian Accounts.

For the Ignacio Utes, this money should be used as a development fund for the individual holdings of the allottees. Their total population was 365, but only the adults now had lands of their own. They were deriving "considerable revenue from their livestock," but the decrease of open range due to the influx of white population gave little hope for the growth of a livestock industry. Their workhorses were of good quality. Much of their land was under irrigation, but more should be cultivated. They needed houses, barns, and home improvements. Several evils held back their development: the availability of liquor, gambling practices, and the extension of credit outside of Federal control.

Davis recommended that the share of capital for the Ute Mountain Utes from the Judgment Fund be applied to buying livestock in the names of individuals. These Indians, being "more nearly in their native state," had little experience of farming, schools, or settled abode. All were still living in tepees or "rude pole huts" (probably summer ramadas). Eight hundred acres, out of less than 1,200 on their reservation deemed suitable for farming, were now under a reclamation project, but they were not being utilized. A few springs on the reservation could be used for irrigation of home garden tracts, but Davis saw the main hope for self-support in the growth of a livestock industry. The tribal range was now mainly being used by white stockmen under grazing permits. Davis thought that with good stallions to improve the Indian pony stock and with herds of cattle and sheep the Ute Mountain Utes could put their own range to more profitable use.

An important proposal in the Davis memorandum on the Ute Judgment Fund was that the Congressional Appropriation should empower the Government to use the fund for the purposes named with or without the consent of the Indians, especially minors and "incompetents" (largely persons who could not speak English or who were illiterate). From tribal funds, additional implements and materials needed for economic growth could be purchased, sold to the Indians as needed, and the proceeds would revert to the original tribal fund. This was the principle of the "Reimbursable Fund," soon to be tested in practice.

Davis foresaw the doubling of the market value of Ute lands if his proposals were made operative. He also foresaw an end to "indolent" life for the Utes, if money advanced to them for specific economic enterprises had to be returned to tribal funds. Cash in the hands of Utes, said Davis, had for years drawn into the area "men of unscrupulous character," seeking to part the Utes from their money and exerting an adverse influence on the entire community.[45] In a separate communication, Davis described the practice of a "Mexican" from Durango of bringing in whiskey on the day when monthly pension checks were distributed to elderly and disabled Utes. On the April 1913 issue day, "several" Indians had become drunk, but the Mexican and a portion of his stock of liquor were seized.[46]

Captain Abbot's comments on the Davis proposals for use of the Ute Judgment Fund were to the effect that sudden changes in the handling of money would be so confusing to the Utes as to have an adverse effect on their economy. He concurred with the Davis proposal to use part of the interest from the Fund for a per capita payment to fulfill Treaty provisions: "The Government should keep to the Treaty or have an understanding with the Indians before making a change. An Indian's mind works very slowly . . . he thinks that any variation from his original interpretation of the treaty means that the white man has lied." For instance, the Utes had been told that their Spring 1913 per capita payment would be "about" $30; when, instead, they received $28.78, they thought that Abbot had pocketed the difference to purchase seed grain. "The Indian should be consulted and should be informed of the changes intended. If he is dissatisfied, he may not work for one or more years, causing a great delay in the progress desired. From my short service I believe that these people must be led and consulted."

Abbot proposed total elimination of per capita payments, if Ute consent could be won, "because they are absolutely incompetent to handle money." He considered the day so remote when they would be capable of self-support that the principal of the Judgment Fund should be kept intact. If Davis's proposal of withdrawing $1,000,000 of principal was approved, Abbot asked that part of the share of the Southern Utes be diverted for establishment of a Home for the aged and helpless, so that these people, some almost blind, would not have their rations shared by young people, as was the current practice. He did not promise that the old people would agree to enter such a Home, but at least the Government would then have done its "duty" by them.

With regard to an Indian Office proposal to place working rations under a reimbursable scheme, Abbot protested that the only condition for receiving such rations should be work. He argued the destitution of the Utes: "The Indians are honest and have paid with this month's annuity old debts they owed to merchants. Some of them are now hungry and without money." Having already made so many changes in arrangements with the Indians, the Government should not try to impose this one: "They feel that the Government is by treaty bound to feed them, and if they are told they will have to pay the Government in work for the ration and work for themselves too, it will be the same to them as paying twice for the ration, and I fear the system would be a failure."[47]

When the reimbursable system was discussed with the Indians, with promises to provide continuing supplies of seed, implements, bulls, and stallions if the Indians would return seed and cash from their annuities at each harvest time, the Utes responded with a marked lack of enthusiasm. Charles Buck remarked that a bull provided the Indians by the Government had been stolen by some white men and that the "Indians did not want any more for the white man to steal." Commented Abbot: "This shows the Indian's method of reasoning."[48]

Shortly thereafter, the newly hired Expert Farmer, S. K. Emerson, requested transfer to the Navajos or Pueblos, "where no rations have ever been issued." As for the Utes, he could not "take these Indians and make prosperous, self-supporting Indian farmers of them, and that, if not this year at least in two years." Explaining Emerson's tone of outrage, Abbot praised the Farmer as long-experienced in the Indian Service and as earnest and kind-hearted, "but Mr. Emerson thinks that cutting down the ration on these people who have been hunters and not farmers does work a hardship." Since the Indians lacked farming ability and sufficient cleared land, even those who did their best to make a living could not make much of a success, especially since the Agency could offer so little paid employment to supplement their incomes.

The lack of success of the working ration system was possibly related to the substitution of fifty pounds of bacon for ninety pounds of beef. A twenty-pound bacon ration was tried first but was recognized as insufficient. Only four men subscribed to the system; a fifth "refused the ration because he wanted articles other than those furnished." (Apparently the Utes, having accepted a diet change from buffalo and venison to beef and mutton, drew the line at bacon). Abbot further remarked that "some of the Indians would just as soon not work and really would prefer not to work." Others, who were working on ditch construction under the Irrigation Engineer, were paid well and needed no interference. Above all, Abbot emphasized his concurrence with Emerson's opinion that the reimbursable system was arousing resistance on the part of the Utes: "The Indians have gotten the idea that they are citizens and can use their money just as it pleases them. This makes it extremely difficult to persuade the Indians to do what we think best."[49, 50]

Along with his resignation, Agency Farmer Emerson submitted figures to prove that economic conditions among the Ignacio Utes were far less rosy than those listed either in the 1912 Annual Report or in the Davis Report. Here are the comparative figures for Ute production and ownership of livestock:

Table 4.1 Comparative Figures for Ute Production and Ownership of Livestock

Products	1912	Davis	Emerson
Oats (bushels)	30,000	20,000	2,000
Wheat (bushels)	7,500	7,500	500
Acres farmed	4,500	4,500	1,200
Horses owned	1,000	1,000	400
Cattle owned	1,500	7,000	100
Sheep owned	not known	2,000	1,000
Goats owned	300	300	400

In submitting his figures, Emerson criticized the impression created by the 1912 Annual report that the gross crop value of the best farmers ranged between $500 and $1,200 apiece and that the average of farm income for all 82 men reported as farming was $500. After checking, Emerson reported that "the high man together with his grown son" had raised only 13 tons of hay, sold at $10 per ton. Another man, the value of whose crops had been listed as $650, had had to buy hay for the use of his stock and had had to keep the 14 sacks of oats he had raised to use for seed in the 1913 planting season.[49]

The Ute Appropriation for F.Y. 1914 was $100,000 instead of the $1,000,000 proposed by Supervisor Davis. Upon this announcement, Superintendent Abbot met at Keams Canyon Indian School with Claude Covey, Superintendent of the Ute Mountain Utes at Navajo Springs, and William Peterson, former Principal of the Fort Lewis School and now Superintendent of Indian Education.

The three drew up a joint "Memorandum Relative to Ute Affairs" which, in essence, supported the proposals of the Davis Report. The pro rata share of the

Ignacio Utes should be placed in Individual Indian Accounts, to be applied for development of farming. The Ute Mountain share should be applied for purchase of stock, development of springs for domestic use, irrigation projects on Ute Mountain, and the improvement of roads. The Joint Memorandum also supported the Davis proposal that the appropriation for Fiscal Year 1915 be $1,000,000 plus accrued interest. Only that portion required by previous treaties should be paid as per capita, the remainder to be used for the benefit of the Utes at the discretion of the Secretary of the Interior. The interest on the $2,000,000 remaining in the Treasury from the Judgment Fund should be applied for supervision of Ute property and for education, but without violating treaties which provided "forever" for benefits, including schools.

Certain additional proposals advanced for the Ignacio Utes were that the condition for Utes to have unrestricted use of their personal shares be the placing under alfalfa of at least 10 acres of an 80-acre allotment. Competent parents should be permitted to manage the funds and property of their minor children. In addition to the above proposals, the Memorandum proposed determination of the rights of the Utes in coal and timberlands disposed of by the Government, for which no compensation had been made to the Indians.

The three administrators proposed that one or two members of each band be placed on a committee to consist of the Superintendents of all three jurisdictions plus one employee each from the Forest Service and the U.S. Geological Survey. The aim would be to reach an agreement with the concurrence of the Indians but, in case concurrence was not achieved, to submit the entire record of transactions to the Secretary of the Interior for his final decision. By this means, additional funds would be provided for the Utes under the direction of the Interior Department.

With regard to the Executive Order providing for an addition to the Ute Mountain reservation, the Memorandum stated that no more reservation land was needed since, with the exception of Mancos Jim's band, little had been done by the unallotted Utes toward self-support. All should be urged to return to the reservation where they were drawing annuities. They should be informed that under Section 4 of the Allotment Act they were entitled to select allotments on the public domain, providing they bore individually the cost of any needed survey.[51]

Shortly before turning the Agency over to incoming Superintendent Walter Runke, Abbot reported a small victory in getting returns on reimbursable articles. In the spring, when he had notified the Indians that all articles issued to them were to be paid for in labor, grain, seed, or cash, some Utes were so incensed that they unloaded plows already placed in their wagons. Later they had relented and taken the reimbursable items. In the fall, Abbot called for labor to cover reimbursable debts. Colorow, son of the former chief, first said he would return the reimbursable articles but later agreed to work as soon as his farm chores were completed. Nate Chase had actually worked three days with his team. "It is a step in the right direction and I am greatly pleased that this has begun before my departure," wrote Abbot.[52]

These hosannas were premature, as the new Superintendent Runke soon discovered. After so many years of receiving rations and annuities, the Utes took kindly neither to the reimbursable system nor to working rations. Cash annuity payments were terminated by the Judgment, and the capital of the Trust Fund set up under the 1874 Agreement was to be distributed pro rata as needed.[53] The combination of withdrawal of previous benefits and what the Utes regarded as the charging of double payment from their own money provoked a groundswell of resistance.

Reporting on the results of the 1913 growing season, cursed by drought, Agency Farmer Emerson reported that when the first efforts were made to impose the reimbursable system on the Utes, "they laid flat down" and, although they did eventually take out the implements and seeds for which they were to pay, it was without enthusiasm. They "compromised in a way and made a half-hearted stagger at farming." Of 59 Indians who took seed, 5 returned it in full or in part at harvest time. Twenty-five percent of the seed was paid for in cash, but some of the Utes who paid at the time of receiving their seed were so severely out of funds during the growing season that they had to leave their crops to run to weeds while they worked on the ditches for wages.

Crudely estimated by stack yards, the hay cut in the 1913 season totalled 687 tons, the amount of each stack being "credited to the head man in the settlement, but in most cases there are 3 or 4 families interested in each of the yards mentioned and depend upon this hay for their pony and horse feed and live together on the returns from any sold." From a 15-ton stack yard, only 3-5 tons would be left for winter feed for an average family string of 6-10 ponies. This was because the families had been forced to sell their summer crop late in the season at $7-10 per ton in order to buy food and clothing. To keep their ponies alive, they would then have to buy hay in the spring at $15-20 per ton.

The situation with regard to water was equally dismal. The Indian farms had suffered during the 1913 dry spell. If 1914 proved equally dry, Emerson predicted "the Mexican, Whiteman and Government employees will get what water they can out of the Pine River and the Indians will get what is left provided their head-gates and ditches are in shape to handle even that little." Emerson reported that, in his first season as Agency Farmer, he had "nothing to do with individual Indian farming operations." His first five weeks had been spent east of the reservation in the Piedra, Cat Creek, Nutra Creek, and Rondo Creek areas, where most of the allotted land was leased to Anglo ranchers.

He had located boundaries, arranged leases, repaired ditches, and tried to regulate irregular timber operations. Emerson had spent another two weeks on the Agency and School hayfields and had also hauled coal and freight to the Agency and School, butchered meat and issued rations, and had put in some time substituting for the Principal and Industrial Teacher during an inspection tour of the Assistant Commissioner of Indian Affairs. None of these activities had advanced the cause of Indian self-support through farming. The part-time help of two Temporary Farmers had had little effect.[54]

It is ironic that at the very moment the Utes were being hailed as "wealthy Indians," they were being pauperized by a premature and, as Emerson believed, senseless drive to propel them to full self-support.

Emerson found that the few families who were "well-nigh self-supporting" and never "bother us much with hard luck stories" were those deriving partial income from successful livestock operations, "equal with the average Mexican or whiteman." He particularly cited the Spencers of Pagosa Junction, who owned 600 sheep and also goats; they also leased land, derived some income from selling timber, and some of the men at times worked on the railroad or on ditches. Emerson listed the family as consisting of 4 men, 5 women, and 3 babies. As in the description of shared income from the sale of hay, Emerson seems here to be describing an economy of sharing from multiple sources of livelihood by an extended family group.

Emerson noted that if tradition and old records were accurate, Ute livestock holdings were on the decline. In cattle, a local predilection for veal shared by all ethnic groups whittled down the number of calves. The Indians tried to keep heifers and had no shortage of bulls, but rigorous winters, feed shortages, and poor care reduced the herds, while the need for ready cash induced more than half of the Indian stock-owners to sell part of their principal stock each year, let alone the increase.

The principal Ute cattle-owners were: Charles Buck (28-30) and James Baker, Rob (Negrito) Richards, Cyrus Grove, and the Johnsons (about 20 apiece). In horses, Charles Buck was again the top owner, with around 50. The Washingtons owned 35, as against the 100 they had owned a few years back. Emerson remarked that of the 60-80 Utes who made any effort to farm or raise a garden, only 6-8 could hitch up a 3-horse team of their own fit to run a grain binder. He felt that if unbroken, healthy mares were kept in tight pasture with the Government and Indian stallions then on hand, ten years of supervised breeding and good care could produce for the Utes "the best horses in America or any other country."

Emerson advocated the fostering of sheep- and goat-raising among the Utes. He predicted success, providing there was exclusive Ute access to a large, unbroken range. Emerson had in mind the Navajo experience, with which he was familiar, and recommended that 500 head of selected sheep and goats be issued to every Indian woman over 18 years of age.[55] While the proposal to turn over the livestock economy to the women was never adopted, it was in line with Agent Weaver's 1877 observation that Ute women and children assumed full care for the livestock and that women had more flexible attitudes than men toward new work patterns.

The 1913 drive for the reimbursable system and for working rations was, predictably, a failure. Superintendent Runke reported at the end of the year that every time he had insisted that an able-bodied man pay in labor for his rations, "it was taken as a huge joke and incomprehensible or he would leave in a huff and remark, we don't want to work for what the Government owes us and are not going to." To get reimbursable cash payments for items that used to be issued free was like "squeezing milk from a turnip."

Runke stated that none of the 150 people receiving part-time rations was able bodied; all were children or aged people. The food they received, however, was promptly shared with "dead-beats and loafers." Runke predicted that if the program were to be applied full-force, the Utes would stop working altogether. He supported their principal demand: continuation of the cash annuity.[56]

Inspecting the allotments along the Pine River, Runke found that many Utes were living on the allotments of friends and relatives rather than on their own. He found great inequality in the value and agricultural potential of the various allotments and proposed the continuing of Werner's concentration policy in the transferring of Indians with poor land to reduced but productive acreages within the Pine River Valley. This program would not affect the Utes living along the Animas and La Plata rivers, since their lands were of better quality.

Before any transfers could be effected, 100 pending heirships to the estates of deceased Utes would have to be settled. These cases would require much work, since most were of long standing and "the Indians, too, have never given the matter of family lineage any thought."[57] It did not occur to Runke that Agency personnel had never attempted to understand Ute categories of kinship which, for instance, assigned mother's sister's daughters to the status of sisters rather than of cousins.

In early 1914, Runke painted a bleak economic and morale situation in a report to the Indian Office: "A disgruntled, half-starved Ute with a few decrepit head of horses or ponies to help in his farm work . . . discouraged because his thin winter diet has sapped the foundation of any ambition. Disgruntled because he feels that the Government is withholding from him what he thinks was faithfully promised to be paid him under their treaty with the United States. Half-starved man and beast because the larder was so often nigh-exhausted."

At best, wrote Runke, the Utes were not fired with the desire to support themselves by work; but tight control over their share of the Judgment Fund was forcing them to seek wage-work on the ditches at the very season when they needed to prepare their lands for planting. He begged for a minimum $15 per capita payment to the 359 Ignacio Utes that spring, more if possible, since the Utes would read into a reduced amount connivance of the Government and Superintendent in appropriating their money "for foreign and private purposes." In conclusion, Runke wrote that he would defer "to the evident desires of the Office." The Utes must be prodded by the pressure of hunger to make greater efforts.[58]

Response from the Indian Office to Runke's assertion that the Ignacio Utes were not ready for full self-support was that they must be made so. Regarding resistance to the Reimbursable system, Runke was informed that the Utes must as of now become accustomed to the condition they would face when Government guardianship was ended: cash payment for goods received.[59] Regarding the reduction in the beef ration, "the Office realizes that the Indians will likely object to this reduction in beef issues, but to accede to their wishes in this matter will only be to continue educating them in the use of beef to the exclusion of other nutritious foods, and will also result in the extravagant use of funds from which they might receive more benefit if otherwise expended."[60]

With regard to the depletion of stock through dwindling of the open range, now largely under the control of Anglo stockmen, Commissioner of Indian Affairs Cato Sells issued an optimistic circular to all Superintendents: "The Indian should be made to realize that the grazing lands of the United States are now almost entirely his own and that he has readily within his reach the possibility of becoming the cattle-, horse-, and sheep-king of America."[61] In view of Washington's disregard for the crushing economic problems the Utes were experiencing, coupled with chronic semi-starvation, it is really surprising that as many as 50 Utes took out seed to plant in the spring of 1914.[62]

The Indian Bill passed by Congress for F.Y. 1915 provided for a $300,000 withdrawal from the principal of the Ute Judgment Fund, of which $100,000 was to be distributed to the Ute Mountain Utes, $200,000 to the Uintah-Ouray group, and nothing to the Ignacio Utes. By the terms of the Bill, the Ignacio Utes received in that year only their pro rata share of accrued interest from the

Judgment Fund, $72,000 to be distributed as $200 payments into 361 Individual Indian Accounts. The inequitable distribution of principal is puzzling in view of the fact that the Judgment was won by all Utes and, furthermore, family ties joined all three jurisdictions, as demonstrated in heirship cases.

Charles Buck complained of unfair treatment to the Southern Utes in an article titled "The Troubles of the Indians," published in the August 1914 issue of *Denver Field and Farm*. The new Superintendent, Walter West, while admitting that the article reflected majority Ute opinion, claimed that the article was ghostwritten, since Buck spoke no English. West said that the opinions expressed had been stimulated by merchants, bootleggers, etc., who stood to "share in the immediate prosperity of the Indians."[63]

In the years from 1913 to 1926, the Ignacio Utes had bank accounts in their own names, some of which were surprisingly large. Only a few "Competent Indians," however, were permitted by the Indian Office to withdraw substantial amounts from these accounts to use on their own, for "betterment" purposes. The Indian Office relied heavily upon the judgment of the Agency Superintendent in recommending withdrawal of sums ranging from $50 to $100 or more from Individual Accounts. In the years during which payments were coming in from the Judgment Fund, Superintendent E. E. McKean mediated the investment of considerable moneys from Individual Indian Accounts in expenditures for "betterment" purposes. In his 1921 Annual Report, McKean expressed confidence that his wise administration of the funds of the Ignacio Utes ensured that by 1925, when the Judgment Fund payments would be terminated, the Utes would be fully self-supporting.[64] What is lacking, however, is evidence that during these years the Utes were given any opportunity to plan and budget their own funds.

Replying to a 1918 Office Circular calling for a report on surplus Indian labor and general economic conditions, McKean stated that "all Indians who will or can work are busy." He gave a rosy picture of conditions in agriculture and stock-raising, indicating that everything was on the upgrade.[65] Yet, when the Ignacio Utes launched charges in 1925-1926 against McKean and the Bureau of Indian Affairs, one of their central accusations was that McKean had for years falsified his reports. They said that their economic conditions had not improved and that exhaustion of the Judgment Fund would leave them destitute.

In an unsigned list of charges presented as a memorandum to the U.S. Senate (to which the Indian Office replied addressing Edwin Taylor and James Baker), particular emphasis was laid on the spending of money which rightly belonged to the Indians "through the medium of bureaucratic control." This meant total control by the Superintendent over transactions made in the names of individual Indians, especially forcing them to sell land against their will and at substandard prices. The memorandum demanded that the Utes have unrestricted control over their own land and money, and that an accounting of their joint funds be made with a view to quick action to save the remainder, "now being squandered at the Agency, through instructions from the Office of the Commissioner of Indian Affairs."[66]

McKean chose to ascribe the explosion of Ute indignation to dismay over the end of annuity payments plus the artful machinations of one José Blas Lucero, of whom more will be said in a later section.[67] The Ute claim that their money had been poured down funnels which brought them no closer to self-support seems to have been accurate.

It has been noted that, over many years, the Utes were apparently responsive to economic arrangements which brought them a clear return. The first such is the symbiotic relationship between Cabezón's band and the Navajos who lived among them; the Utes shared the Navajos' corn and the Navajos shared the Utes' hunting spoils. In the late 1880s, 32 Ute farms were in operation with Hispanic farmers working them on half-shares and the Ute employers enjoying half the harvest. These were informal and voluntary arrangements, encouraged by Agent Stollsteimer, who had close ties with the Hispanos. Share-agreements continue to the present despite generations of Agency disapproval of Hispanic share-farmers and insistence that the Ignacio Utes work their farms alone. Yet the Utes found that the employment of share-farmers brought them modest subsistence and growing improvements, and this practice encouraged them to settle down voluntarily to farming life in the Hispanic pattern. Share agreements even worked successfully in reverse, as seen in José Velásquez's employment of Utes on shares in cattle-raising. Again, the Utes willingly undertook short-term wage jobs, as seen not only in the years of springtime activity on ditch repairs, but also in the record of youths sent in Superintendent Werner's time to work at Rocky Ford under contracts arranged by the Supervisor of Indian Employment. In a sequence of years, employers asked for the return of youths previously employed, stating that their work had been satisfactory and promising to send them to the local public schools.[68]

Despite the above evidence that numerous Utes were able and willing to work according to a variety of established local patterns, Captain Abbot completely dismissed the possibility that the Utes could work at wages, at least in the San Juan Basin. He likened the attitude of local ranchers toward the Indians to that of townsmen toward soldiers in an Army camp: "The merchants and farmers will squeeze every cent out of the Indians they can, and when they have done this they have no further use for them."[69]

When Runke was Superintendent, he expressed reluctance to send young school-trained Utes on jobs off the reservation, especially to the coal mines near Durango, lest they be exposed to "booze" and "vices."[70] No Superintendent seems to have taken note that the small Anglo and Spanish ranchers had to work out at wages periodically to make ends meet, and that the same practice might have advanced the cause of self-support for the much less skilled and dedicated Ute farmers. Determination to keep the Utes' noses to the ground on their own farms seems to have outweighed any other consideration, especially during the years of World War I. Then Superintendent McKean's patriotic fervor led to his assertion that the Ignacio Ute farmers were contributing to the national bread-basket and should be excused from Army Service.[71]

Summary

To complete the Narrative Section without drawing premature conclusions, this point should be made. Four larger issues were selected to serve as focal points of the narrative:

- *removal*, that is, the forcible relocation of Indians,
- *allotment*, that is, the division of formerly communal lands into private holdings,
- *the land and water question*, which arose from allotment, and
- *the conflicting, and sometimes ethically conflicted interests of administrators*, expressed in varying policies on the above as well as in provision of rations, stock and seed, the hiring of Indians, and the approach toward sharecropping by Hispanos on Ute lands.

These served as some of the stimuli for and against change during the first fifty years of Agency operation. Many other stimuli existed. These four, however, are the issues best documented in the FRC records. They appear also to provide a foundation for analyzing the nature of changes in Ute life over the fifty-year span and of the contact relations under which they occurred.

Chapter 5
Statistics of Change

The statistical tables on the following pages were compiled from Reports of the Commissioner of Indian Affairs (ARCIA) and records from the Denver Federal Records Center for the years indicated.[1] It will be noted that it is difficult to compare figures for sequences of years starting in the 1880s and continuing to 1921. Although the total population of the 1880s is subdivided to identify the Muwaches and Kapotas, who together later formed the bulk of the allotted Ignacio Utes, there is no corresponding subdivision in livestock holdings and other parameters for those years.

It should also be noted that the first year for which the figures refer exclusively to the allotted Ignacio Utes is 1905, since in the early post-allotment years the Utes of southwestern Colorado were not administratively subdivided. The notation for 1878 excludes the Muwaches, most of whom were still receiving rations at the Maxwell Ranch in northeastern New Mexico. Many of them at that time spent their summers with the Jicarilla Apaches camping at the Great Sand Dunes in the San Luis Valley of southwestern Colorado.

Table 5.1 Vital Statistics

A. Population: Wiminuch, Muwach, Kapota, and Combined total

Year	Population	Births	Deaths	# Farming	# Stockraising	# Houses
1878	786 (total)[a]	27	12	0		0
1884	991 (total)	35	27	15		4
	498W[b]					
	286M					
	207K					
1886	978 (total)	33	46	28	156 Families	7
	498W					
	286M					
	199K					
1891	978 (total)	32	46	30		5 (occupied)
1899	396 allotted	16	19		90 Families	40
	622 unallotted					

[a] In 1878, 44 Navajos were enrolled with the Wiminuch, becoming Ute tribal members.
[b] W: Wimenuch. M: Muwach. K: Kapota.

68

Table 5.1 Vital Statistics (continued)

B. Ignacio Utes Only

Year	Population	Births	Deaths	Allotted Farmers	Unallotted	# Houses
1905	ca. 385	10	8	40 Families		40
1911	362	23	13	41 Families	39 Adults 142 Minors	43
1921	329	8	13	69 (out of 115 with allotments)	214 Total[c] 24 farming	78

[c]In 1921, Agency records recorded the total number of unallotted families and stated that 24 farmed.

Table 5.2 Livestock Owned by Utes

A. Wiminuch-Muwach-Kapota Combined

Year	Horses	Horses and Mules	Mules	Sheep	Sheep and Goats	Goats	Cattle	Poultry
1884	2,000		50	3,500[a]			150	
1886	3,700		72		5,400		246	
1891	4,500		50	1,500		2,000	500	
1899		2,038		2,400		900	75	100

B. Ignacio Utes Only

Year	Horses	Horses and Mules	Mules	Sheep	Sheep and Goats	Goats	Cattle	Poultry
1905	800[b]		50	3,000		1,500	150	150
1911		1,464					1,720	1,150
1921		525		510		320	289	630

[a] Including 1,500 remaining from 4,800 that U.S. Government gave in 1883.
[b] 300 had been sold.

Table 5.3 Property and Livelihood

A. Acreage and Usage of Ignacio Allotments (1896-1921)

Year	Number of Allotments	Total Acres	Irrigated Acres	Acres Worked by Utes	Leased Acres
1896	371 + 4 double allotments	72,811 + 1,280			
1899	375			400	
1905	375			800	
1911	375	73,120	4,080	4,080	1,719
1921	237	50,938	14,720	19,700	9,200

B. Value of Property Owned by Ignacio Utes (1911-1921)

Year	Land	Livestock	Houses, Equipment, Furnishings, etc.	Individual Indian Accounts	Total
1911	$87012.80	$72,310	$16,000	$40,445.45	$229,529
1921	$412,700	$54,445	$33,500	$78,420	$567,365

Table 5.4: Ratio of Self-Support to Dependency

A. Wiminuch-Muwach-Kapota Combined

Year	Population	Hunting/Gathering	Farming	Stockraising	On Rations
1886	978	26%	54%	156 families	20%
			28 families		

B. Ignacio Utes Only

Year	Population				
1905	385	75% "Civilized Pursuits"		25%	
1911	362	Totally self-supporting-50	Partly self supporting-100	On Rations-280	
1921	329	Totally self-supporting-6	Partly self supporting-232	On Rations-98	

72

Table 5.5 Education

A. Wiminuch–Muwach–Kapota Combined

Year	School-age Children	Attendance at: Agency	Day/Boarding	Public/Outside Boarding	Literate	Speak English
1884	316			24	24	24
1886	267	14			24	40
1891	218				14	35

B. Ignacio Utes Only

1905	114		70		12	75
1911	90[a]	23	60	8	57[b]	102
1921	102[c]	31	46	17	60	95

[a] Plus 11 not attending.
[b] Figure for 1912.
[c] Plus 15 not attending.

73

Chapter 6
Elements of Contact Relations

In the years 1877-1926, the stable contact maintained by the Utes of Southwestern Colorado with other groups was a key factor in the relatively complex patterns of change. In the first place, the Utes had access to a wider range of acculturative choices than projected in the U.S. Government program of directed culture change. In the second place, multiple inter-group contacts reduced the influences coming from the Agency as well as from the economically and politically dominant group, the Anglo-Americans. Following are the contact elements and the nature of the contact relations.

"Washington" and the Agency

Congress, with its committees and appointed commissions, and the Department of the Interior-Indian Office-Ignacio Agency staff formed echelons with, on one hand, legislative power to enact and, on the other, executive power to carry out policies with regard to the Utes. These bodies represented a formidable array of power, but the Utes learned early to maneuver between them, pitting one echelon against another, thus reducing pressure on themselves.

When gathered to the reservation in 1877, the Utes had not experienced concerted military action and a series of crushing defeats, such as were inflicted on the Cheyennes and Sioux, for instance. The only serious encounter had been the engagements of Colonel Fauntleroy against the Muwaches in the winter of 1854-1855. The fact that the Muwach and Kapota Utes came to the reservation without military escort, which had been planned in order to force them to move from New Mexico,[1] is no doubt emblematic of the Utes' awareness that resistance was futile, but this did not mean that they arrived in broken and beaten condition. On the contrary, from the outset, they made their demands heard.

In ensuing years, no decisions were made by the Government without some concessions to Ute demands. For instance, the work-for-rations ruling of 1875 was shelved at their insistence and was never fully implemented. The allotment-or-removal controversy of the first 18 years was affected by the tactics of Ute factions. In successive periods, Utes lodged complaints against Agency personnel before the Indian Office and, in turn, against the Indian Office before the Interior Department or Congressional committees.

While the ties of some Agency personnel with local interests at times increased pressure upon the Utes, they also at times caused Agency leaders to forget or to modify directives from Washington. For years, Utes could elude Agency control by shifting their campsites. In the low-population area of the reservation and its surroundings, the whereabouts of individual Utes could remain unknown for years, even when issue of rations and annuities drew most Utes to the Agency.

Over the 50-year period, 22 Agents and Superintendents succeeded one another at the Agency, with equal turnover of clerks and other personnel. Few knew more than a handful of Utes.

Before the 1910 Judgment, direct and primary control over the Utes was exercised by the Agency through issuing of rations and annuities. Afterwards, the administration of Individual Indian Bank Accounts became the means of control. While the purpose of the Agency was to guide changes leading to self-support among the Utes, its functions perpetuated dependency.

Non-Utes on or Near the Reservation

In 1877, a permanent population of Anglos, Hispanos, Navajos, Paiutes, and Jicarilla Apaches lived in the area surrounding the Southern Ute reservation. In the early years, the following can be stated in general of these diverse population elements:

- Anglos continually sought to have the Utes removed to Utah.
- Hispanos sought to benefit from employment by and activities with the Utes.
- Individual Navajos, Paiutes, Apaches, and also some Pueblo Indians were, with Ute concurrence, included on the Ute tribal rolls.
- Along the ill-defined western border of the reservation, Navajos and Paiutes ranged in shifting contact with Ute encampments.
- The Jicarillas, headquartered at Dulce, New Mexico, near the southeast border of the Ute reservation, were in frequent contact.

The Anglos, from the outset, dominated ranching, politics, and social relations along the northern and western peripheries of the reservation. As in most frontier communities of the time, there was a noticeable lawless element, spurred by anti-Indian sentiment. Much has been said in chapter 2 about the shooting forays of the 1880s at the western end of the reservation; less hostile but equally lawless contact was mediated in the same period by bootlegging operations. In early 1887, L. M. Armstrong covered the area west of Ute Mountain as a detective investigating the liquor trade with the Utes. He reported to Agent Stollsteimer: "There is some hard characters in this country, you bet."[2]

The Utes ranging the western end of the reservation had little non-Indian contact except with Anglos. It is no doubt for this reason that by 1890 the Wiminuches were described as more advanced in learning English than the Muwaches and Kapotas.[3]

Social contact with Anglos was minimal and the Utes seemed content to leave it so. After allotment, the Ute Mountain segment reduced contact with their Anglo neighbors, perhaps because they felt that those who had advised them had given poor advice. Deepening isolation was a factor in the cultural conservatism which, for years, gave the unallotted Utes the reputation of being the least friendly and most "backward" of all Utes.

From the first, neighboring Anglos strenuously tried to limit the rights and privileges of the Utes and the Utes, just as strenuously, held the line, sometimes calling for military protection, just as the Anglos did and perhaps for better reason. In 1887, word came from the Uintah and Ouray Agency that the people of Colorado had "served notice that they would shoot down all Indians that they see across the line of the reservation."[4] In later years, the same intemperance was expressed less savagely. When Moav reported that the son of a Bayfield man had shot his heifer, the father retorted: "he is badly mistaken and if he was a white man I would have him arrested for making false reports or if you will show me a white man that will say what you said Moab said I will give you [$]25.00."[5]

Agency policy operated to keep Utes and Anglos from wrangling, but especially to avoid situations in which Utes seemed to have authority over Anglos, even on their own reservation. With regard to the use of Indian Police, Agent Page said in 1881: "I have not deemed it practicable to attempt their use where it was probable that they would be brought into contact with whites."[6] The authority of Indian Police to drive trespassing livestock off reservation lands continued to be a delicate question for years. In later times, Superintendent McKean vetoed a proposal that Utes be employed as ditch riders to halt the illegal diversion of irrigation water: "Our ditches here supply water to the Whites and Indians alike and there are many occasions for efficient administration and the employment of much tact in administering the general affairs of the water distribution."[7]

Although the acculturative model held up before the Utes by the Agency was that of the Anglo rancher, few Utes through 1926 showed much inclination to emulate this model. But the Utes attached to the Ignacio Agency, living from the eastern limit of the reservation to the La Plata River, accepted in varying degrees the model provided by their Hispanic neighbors.

There is no documentary evidence that before 1877 there were any permanent Hispanic settlers living in the area immediately adjacent to the reservation other than the Durango miners who formed an enclave within the area of Anglo control. According to tradition, some of the earliest miners had come from the northern states of Mexico and did not develop relations with the Utes.

Within a few months of the foundation of the Agency, however, and apparently in direct response to its existence, Hispanic Americans from communities in northern New Mexico and from the San Luis Valley of southwestern Colorado began to arrive.

From the seventeenth century, there had been Hispano-Ute contact. The Utes, alone or in the company of other Indians such as Comanches, had intermittently raided the northern fringe communities of Hispanic settlement but had also enjoyed trade relations and brief alliances with the Hispanos. Among the earliest Hispanic settlers near the reservation, some had known from childhood Ute children raised in their homes. These were officially designated as "captives" but in some instances where data are available, it would appear that they had been voluntarily handed over by their parents in exchange for food and stock. They had been baptized, raised in Hispanic fashion, and they and their progeny were addressed in kin terms by the members of the Hispanic households. Some married Hispanic spouses.

Among the first Hispanic settlers of the San Juan Basin, Francisco Manzanares was of Ute birth but raised in "captivity" in the lower Chama Valley. He brought his Hispanic wife and their grown children. They homesteaded Turley, which was then called Alcatraz because of the storks that nested by the nearby river. José Salomé Jáquez, a Hispano who had been raised as a "captive" of the Utes accompanied Manzanares. Since both men spoke Ute and were known to Ute leaders, they were treated as friends. Thomas Burns, the leading merchant of Tierra Amarilla warmly recommended a member of this group, Juan N. Valdez, as one who had been "interpreter for the Utes for a great many years . . . a man in whom you can put full confidence under any circumstances."[8] The Utes, mostly Wiminuches at the time, expressed preference for the services of Valdez over those of the Kapota leader, Severo.[9]

As soon as the reservation was established, members of the Valdez family, along with their Manzanares, Vallejos, and other kin, came up from their homesteads to work on the reservation as herders, construction laborers, and tenants on the pre-allotment farms, and also did so in most subsequent years. In the post-allotment years and particularly following the 1910 Judgment, these same lineages settled permanently in the Ignacio area and were active in running Ute farms and building Indian homes. Their relations with the Utes were cordial. They often shared Ute encampments or houses and became warmly acquainted.

Other Hispanic settlers arrived in 1878 and located within the reservation line near the later site of Arboles, Colorado. Removed by troops in early 1883, they converged on the nearby hamlet of Rosa, New Mexico, on the east bank of the San Juan River, just below its confluence with the Piedra.

Some of these settlers were not sure of their reception by the Utes. A log house still standing in Rosa in the summer of 1961 was supposedly one which was brought from Walsenberg, disassembled on an ox-cart and reassembled in Rosa to serve as a fort in case of trouble. Until 1890 some other Rosa residences were of the same defensive type.

These anxieties, however, appear to have had little foundation. Through the 1880s, Hispanic settlement spread without incident along the west bank of the San Juan at the southern fringes of the reservation. From the early 1880s, settlement also spread up the Pine River from its confluence with the San Juan until by the early post-allotment period it was discovered that some Hispanic homesteads were on Ute land.

From their first appearance, the Hispanos were a thorn in the side of the Agency leadership because of their liquor shops and their willingness to do business with the Utes. The López bar near Arboles provoked the survey of the reservation line which led to the ouster of the Arboles settlers.[10]

From the Ute point of view, however, recreational possibilities in the Hispanic settlements were attractive and Utes reciprocated by giving Hispanic stockmen preferential use of their range at little or no cost, freeing them for many years from competition with Anglo stockmen for the use of open range. Rosa became a mercantile center for the expanding sheep industry of the area.

Some Hispanic stockmen, according to tradition, won their first sheep in the drinking and gambling sprees which followed each annuity payment. Utes and many other Indians from the Jicarilla and Navajo reservations attended the Rosa fiestas and were participants in horse-races, gambling, and other diversions.

The apogee of Rosa's fortunes as an independent Hispanic community was reached around 1910, after which a slow decline in the sheep industry began, due in part to the reduction of Ute range. The largest store, after 1910, fell progressively under the control of a financially powerful group of Anglo creditors who, within a few years, became full owners. Following the enactment of the Colorado Prohibition law in 1916 and the National Prohibition law in 1918, the principal enterprise of Rosa became moonshining and bootlegging operations. Between 1916 and 1918, thirsty Colorado residents could go to Rosa and enjoy a drink in one of its seven bars, conveniently located just south of the state line, but after enactment of National Prohibition (the Volstead Act) in 1919, such transactions became illegal.

    In the early years, no Agent with the exception of Christian Stollsteimer is
known to have set foot in Rosa, so that for years Agency comments on the
nefarious influence of the little hamlet upon the Utes were based on hearsay.
Later actions against bootlegging operations were undertaken by Federal
Agents, but from first to last it proved difficult to bar the Utes from illegal liquor
transactions. They protected their whiskey supply from whatever source by
refusing to serve as witnesses in court proceedings against the suppliers, causing
many liquor cases to be dismissed for insufficient evidence.[11]

    Other settlements which brought together Hispanos and Utes were La Posta
on the Animas River, settled by 1890 if not before, also a scattering of ranches
up the Piedra River, where stockmen began to buy "vacant" Ute allotments at
the turn of the century, and Ignacio, which had a substantial Hispanic population
when it became a township in 1910.

    The cultural influence of the Hispanos upon the Utes from 1877 to 1926
was, as it had been ever since the seventeenth century, conducted under
conditions of loose symbiosis without dominance of one group over the other.
Despite occasional quarrels between individuals, the prevailing atmosphere was
one of social harmony based upon mutual economic interest. The widest
influence was undoubtedly exerted by those Hispanos who actually lived among
Utes and worked with and for them. These included few Agency regular
employees but numerous "temporaries." After allotment, such influence spread,
not alone among the Ignacio Utes but also, to an extent, among the Ute
Mountain Utes who employed Hispanic sheepmen.

    In the early years following allotment, a few Hispanic farmers were
employed at Ignacio, but in 1903 an inspector recommended their discharge on
the grounds that some of the Ignacio Utes had demanded their replacement by
Anglos. It was alleged that "the Indians say they (the Hispanos) own ranches of
their own near the reservation and spend more time on them than they do in
assisting and instructing the Indians." The Commissioner of Indian Affairs
appeared to support the inspector's recommendation that Nicolás Jeantet and his
assistants, Antonio Trujillo and Luis Martínez, be discharged from Agency
employ.[12]

    The implications of the above statements are belied by the long record of
Ute compatibility with Hispanic farmers. More likely, it reflects the fact that, by
the early 1900s, an increasing number of Utes were preferentially obtaining
Agency employment in ranks previously open to Hispanic employees. This
possibility is underlined by the Commissioner's 1904 instructions to Agent
Smith to discharge J. V. Manzanares as Assistant Farmer and Ben Manzanares
as Teamster on the following grounds: "As these positions are created for

Indians, Mexicans cannot be employed."[13] Ironically, the two Manzanares men may well have been descendants of a Ute, Francisco Manzanares.

In that same year, the number of Indian Police Privates was reduced from 12 to 5, so that those Ignacio Utes who had become accustomed to a steady wage had to look for new employment.[14] Yet throughout the years, Agency employment for the Utes was seldom of long duration, between resignations and dismissal for "insubordination, neglect of duty or health reasons."[15]

Another reason the Agency gave for its reluctance to hire Hispanic employees was a low opinion of their influence on Ute work habits, as highlighted in the José Velásquez case, previously discussed in some detail in chapter 5. The real objection seems to have been that Hispanic employees did not put the required degree of pressure upon the Utes to hustle, but rather worked with them at their own pace. An example is provided by the case of José (Benito) Ulibarrí who was employed as Stockman for some years at Ute Mountain. In 1925, he was described as a congenial family man of good habits whose "work among the Indians has resulted in advancement of the Indians in the sheep industry." Superintendent McKean recommended, however, that Ulibarrí be replaced by a more "progressive and dynamic" Stockman (in the Anglo-Protestant style), one who could match him in knowledge of sheep but who "has the faculty of interesting the Indians in this work and has such principles of discipline as is absolutely necessary for successful work among these Indians."[16]

Despite the low numbers of official Hispanic Agency employees, the number of Hispanos involved in stockwork, clearing of land, building Ute homes and, especially, operating the farms of the Ignacio Utes, apparently increased rather than decreased over the years. It is amusing that, while the last Superintendent to mention even casually such operations was Walter Runke, at least one modern informant stated positively of his own experience that Fabián Martínez, famous in the FRC records as a bootlegger, enjoyed for years a profitable agreement with Superintendent McKean to provide Hispanic labor for home building and tenant farming among the Ignacio Utes.

Steady and friendly contact between Ignacio Utes and their Hispanic neighbors at work and play continued with occasional Hispanic-Ute intermarriages before 1926. A few "Mexican women" of easy virtue were credited with the introduction of venereal diseases, first noted in the late 1880s.[17] Tradition has it that a few Hispanic individuals were so eager to secure annuities and allotments that they tried to pass themselves off as Utes.

Hispanic land hunger and interest in Ute money may possibly have motivated a few marriages. It appears more significant, however, that with one known exception all early intermarriages were contracted with a Ute partner who had been reared in a Hispanic home and was a practicing Catholic. All such Utes as are known in the records, in fact, married either Hispanic spouses or Indians who had been raised like themselves.

There was thus from the earliest years of the reservation a small percentage of Utes who were particularly adapted to Hispanic ways. This percentage was reinforced and expanded by the existence of the mixed Hispanic-Ute community of La Posta on the Animas River from the early 1890s. In the vicinity lived the Head-Tucsón-Vásquez-Mestas-Casías kindred, who later intermarried with Raels, Montoyas, Trujillos, Vigils, and other families; they also intermarried with the Weaselskin or William family and the family of Corup Charlie Chávez (christened Juan Manuel García) with several adopted children. In this community full-Utes and part-Utes were enrolled in the tribe while participating in a community organized along Hispanic lines. In 1917, the public school teacher of La Posta was not sure if the adopted part-Indian daughter of Charlie Chávez was Ute or Hispanic, and she described her Ute and Hispanic pupils as being very much alike, both in their excellent deportment at school and in their shyness about reciting before the class.[18]

Some features of Hispanic kin organization were parallel to traditional Ute practice: the barring of marriage with a first cousin (*primo hermano* in Spanish, suggesting a semi-sibling status); frequent rearing of children by their grandparents; emphasis upon seniority among siblings and also within consanguineal lines; preferential matrilocal residence of recently married couples; eagerness to adopt children. Exclusively Hispanic features which were adopted by the Utes and part-Utes of La Posta derived from integration into a Catholic community. They included the kin-religious functions of baptismal godparents and wedding sponsors and, at least until 1926, permanent marriage ties.

To conclude the review of Ute-Hispanic contact relations, it can be observed that they ranged from a voluntary and partial assimilative trend reflected in marriages to much more casual relations mediated by work and recreational activities. Social intimacy and the continued use of both Spanish and Ute as contact languages was fortified by the presence of Hispanic children, assumed by the authorities to be part-Indian, at the Fort Lewis School in the 1890s. In fact, at this school, as at the Presbyterian School of the Rev. A. J. Rodríguez in Ignacio from 1894 to the early 1900s, there seem to have been more Hispanic than Ute students. Only a portion of Ute-Hispanic contact was under Agency direction, and some of it was contrary to Indian Policy.

Turning now to non-Ute Indians on or near the reservation, it must first be observed that it is not clear just how many of the "Utes" on the first annuity rolls were, in fact, Navajos, Jicarillas, Paiutes, or Indians from other groups. There were, supposedly, 44 Navajos in Cabezón's band. Through the 1880s, the FRC records reflect Agency uncertainty as to which Indians roaming the area west of Ute Mountain were Utes and which were Paiutes. Of the 150 "renegades" who were added to the tribal rolls in 1895, it can be guessed that some were indeed Paiutes.

Under the 1868 Treaty, any "friendly" Indians whom the Utes might choose to admit to their reservation were to be included in the benefits of the Treaty. That the Utes did so choose is clear. Luis Ortiz (Job Cooper) was a Taos Indian married to a Ute woman; their 1895 allotment was made in his name and after the wife died without issue, Ortiz married a Taos woman whose children by him became heirs to the allotment.[19]

To the uncertain number of non-Ute Indians who were actually on the reservation at the time of its founding must be added the annual appearance over the years of Navajos and Jicarillas who worked for the Agency at road and ditch work as well as for neighboring ranchers and stockmen. A number of Navajo herders were employed, especially by the Ute Mountain Utes, but also by some of the Ignacio Utes. At Ignacio, there is a record of some marriages of these Navajos with Ute women.

Contact with Paiutes was mainly limited to the Ute Mountain area. The Ignacio Utes appear to have had the main contacts with Jicarillas, while Navajo contact spread over the entire reservation. What the FRC records in no way reveal is the nature of changes, if any, effected upon Ute culture by any of these contacts. Navajo ambivalent attitudes toward twin births may have spread to the Utes. Both Navajo and Pueblo ancestors of part-Ute families were well known to Hispanos of the 1960s; they were remembered as fluent in Spanish and familiar with Hispanic ways. The most famous ancestral Navajos among the Utes were James Baker and Steven Burch.

Non-Local Indians

Between the Northern Utes and the Utes of southwestern Colorado, there existed bonds of cultural identity and blood kinship which were constantly renewed by visits and by transfer of individuals and families from one jurisdiction to another. These transfers continued well beyond the allotment years and were often preceded by years of living away from the jurisdiction of allotment. By living away from their allotments, many Utes both of Utah and of southwestern Colorado escaped pressure to take up farming. Their allotments were leased and they lived on the income therefrom plus their annuities. In this sense, it can be said that relations between Northern and Southern Utes acted as a barrier to the program of directed culture change.

Both Northern and Southern Utes maintained a broad network of contact with other tribes of Plains culture and shared between them the results of such contact, notably in the field of religious thought.

The FRC records shed little light on the spread of the Ghost Dance, Sun Dance, and Peyote Religion among the tribes in contact; yet it can hardly be doubted that the amicable relations which developed between the Northern Utes,

Red Cloud's Sioux, and the Wind River Shoshones on the one hand, and between the Southern Utes, Kiowas of Anadarko, and Cheyennes-Arapahos of Darlington, Oklahoma, on the other were connected with the spread of these cults among both Northern and Southern Utes. Several documents in the Federal Records hint of such connections.[20]

Omer C. Stewart's *Peyote Religion: A History*[21] is an authoritative study of the origins and spread of the Native American Church, while Joseph G. Jorgensen's *The Sun Dance Religion: Power for the Powerless*[22] traces the origins and significance of this spiritual manifestation. Neither book focuses closely upon the Southern Ute experience but the information provided is applicable.

Despite the lack of data in the FRC records, it does seem clear that the Utes of southwestern Colorado were both selective and economical in adopting new features from other tribes. The Ghost Dance, described by Opler as a brief and unsuccessful borrowing,[23] receives no mention in the FRC records. The Sun Dance, in the years up to 1926, did not achieve full annual regularity of observance.[24]

The Peyote Religion early on acquired few Ignacio Ute adherents. On the other hand, these latter were described as being "of the better class, both from the point of industry and abiding by the law."[25] There is here no implication of a revivalist movement led by acculturative die-hards, but rather of a prestigious and somewhat expensive innovation by those who could best afford it.

Chapter 7
Categories of Change

Changes in the systems under which the culture of the Utes of southwestern Colorado operated from 1877 to 1926 can be traced in the FRC records in the fields of economics, politics, education and, to an extent, in medical-religious practices. Beyond these categories, the data are neither full nor direct; for instance, the functions of kin groups can be dimly perceived through such data as heirship proceedings and records of Individual Indian Accounts, but the arbitrary and inconsistent use of English names for Utes often obscured close kin ties. It is hard on the basis of these records to project a clear picture of changes in kin functions.

Economic Change

The 1877 program outlined by Carl Schurz[1] focused on the following changes to be effected in the economy of the Western Plains Indians:

1) Nomadism was to be replaced by fixed residence.
2) Hunting-gathering subsistence was to be replaced by farming and stockraising.
3) Individual enterprise was to be stimulated.
4) Acquisition of private property in land and money was to be promoted.

Data for changes under Schurz's headings follow.

Fixed Residence

Fixed residence was a pre-condition to effective operation of this program, as first underlined by Agent Francis Weaver in his comments on the "nomadic mania" of the Utes. He predicted that they would never change their ways so long as they continued to move about at will and, furthermore, he noted that many who had not previously lived under the direct control of an Agency that wished to remain at the furthest possible remove on the reservation, where Agency control would remain a fiction.[2]

The building of houses for influential Utes was commenced in 1884[3] and, although the reluctance of the Utes to live in anything but tepees or brush shelters was frequently mentioned in subsequent years, the Ignacio Utes were reported as having 40 dwellings "occupied" in 1905.[4] In the years following the 1910 Judgment, quite a number of houses were built for Ignacio Utes, paid for from Individual Indian Accounts. The 1921 Annual Report lists 78 houses for a total of 124 Ignacio Ute "heads of families," whereas the Ute Mountain Utes are described as still living largely in tents and brush shelters.[5] Yet houses belonging to Ignacio Utes are not proof positive of permanent residence in them, if the recollection of living informants for the mid-twenties is considered. They say that a majority of the Ignacio Utes lived, at least during the summer, in canvas tents and brush shelters and that their houses were often occupied by Hispanic share tenants or leasers.

Aside from the data on dwellings, the FRC records provide abundant evidence for continuing mobility. After allotment, prolonged visits by Ignacio Utes to the Utah jurisdiction and elsewhere kept them for years suspended between Agencies. Enrollment transfers sometimes had to be held up for years while their whereabouts were being checked. In 1909, after the White River Utes had returned to the Uintah Agency following a stay in South Dakota, the Agent there had a hard time catching up with Sue Clay to complete the cancellation of some Clay allotments at Ignacio. He commented sourly, "these runaway Indians upon their return have scattered themselves to a considerable extent."[6] In 1917, Corson, Abigail, and Susan Dickinson had been missing for over nine years and, when Superintendent McKean inquired about them at the Navajo Springs Agency, the laconic reply was: "The last heard of them they left this reservation for Pine River."[7]

It can only be concluded that fifty years of reservation life had not extinguished Ute mobility, even among the "settled" Ignacio Utes. This fact is relevant to other aspects of economic change.

Changes in Subsistence Economy

Changes in subsistence economy have been partly described in chapter 5 on self-support. In analyzing the changes, we must remember that, despite changing means of subsistence, the Utes of southwestern Colorado were not more economically dependent upon the Government in 1926 than in 1877, nor yet were they more fully self-supporting.

In 1881, Agent Page described the means for self-subsistence: the annual fall hunt for big game provided dried meat for winter provisions. Hides were dressed and sold or exchanged for trade goods. Most Utes owned horses and, in addition, some kept small herds of sheep and goats which they slaughtered for food when deep snows prevented them from reaching the Agency to collect rations. Cabezón, the Wiminuch sub-chief, sometimes sold a few cows to the Agency butcher from his herd of over a hundred.[8]

In 1887, Agent Stollsteimer estimated that the Utes derived 40% of their subsistence by hunting, 40% from their sheep and goats, and 20% from Government support. He did not mention the tenant farms on the Pine River, but stated that about half the Utes were engaged in farming and the other half in stockraising. Stock owned was estimated at 5,000 horses, 400 cattle, 1,000 goats, and 3,000 sheep. Only three individuals owned very much stock and Stollsteimer added that the Utes cared little to be rich.[9] This estimate conflicts with that of 1886, for which the corresponding ratios are 26% - 54% - 20%.[10]

By the early 1920s, statistical reports indicate many changes in the subsistence activities of the Ignacio Utes, but the fact that degree of self-support had not vastly altered is suggested by the figures on rations over the years. In the pre-allotment years, rations were given to all but, as has been noted, the Utes had other sources of food supply through the men's hunting activities and the food-gathering activities of the women.

By 1900, the annual cost of rations for all Utes of southwestern Colorado was less than half that of the national average for all Indians and only about one-quarter the cost of full rations. It appears, however, that most were receiving some rations.[11] In 1905, it was estimated that 75% of the subsistence of the Ignacio Utes was derived from "civilized pursuits" and only 25% from rations but, again, there is no evidence that the number receiving part rations had been reduced.[4]

In 1911, out of a total population of 362 Ignacio Utes, 238 able-bodied adults and also 39 minors and disabled persons were receiving rations for which they performed no labor. In view of the fact that few Ignacio minors were in boarding schools in that period, these 39 children must have constituted the majority of all Ute school-age minors. By 1912, upon Indian Office insistence that only minors and disabled adults receive rations for which no labor was performed, the total of able-bodied adults receiving rations without labor fell to 140, but the number of minors and disabled on rations rose to 80.

By 1921, with a total population of 329, no adults listed as able-bodied were receiving rations, but there were 82 adults listed as disabled and 16 minors on the ration roll. In this year there were a number of Ute boarding school students, including some who were over age 18, hence technically adults, so that the total number of Ignacio Utes on their home grounds was reduced. The rise in the numbers of "disabled," therefore, might reflect a re-definition of the term to keep landless Utes from starving. The drop in the annual beef ration from 96,000 pounds in 1911 to 33,484 pounds in 1912 and 16,947 pounds in 1921 gives no proof of the exact degree of self-support but rather implies that more

Ignacio Utes were near starvation in 1921 than in 1911.[5, 12, 13] Certainly, the continuing high proportion of Ignacio Utes receiving supplementary food belies the glowing Agency reports on growing prosperity in the early twenties.

Certain comparative figures for 1911 and 1921 actually indicate economic decline. Whereas in 1911 there were still 375 allotments at Ignacio, with 181 living owners, by 1921 the number of allotments had dwindled to 237 and only 115 had living owners. Ignacio Utes owning no allotments in 1911 numbered 39 adults and 142 minors and in 1921 the total number of non-owners on the Ignacio rolls had risen to 214. Horse ownership had declined from 1,450 in 1911 to slightly over 500 in 1921. There had been a rise in the number of sheep and goats owned, yet the total value of Ute-owned livestock had dropped from $72,310 in 1911 to $54,445 in 1921. Ironically, total deposits in Individual Indian Bank Accounts had risen from $40,446.45 in 1911 to $76,420 in 1921, yet there is no firm evidence that the Utes had achieved either a higher standard of living or a sounder basis for self-support in the intervening decade.[5, 13]

Informant recollection fills in gaps in the FRC records for these years, when allotments in land and the proceeds of the Judgment Fund were heralded in Agency reports as a sure guarantee of future Ute affluence. Informants recall that the Ignacio men continued to hunt and the women continued gathering foodstuffs, though apparently these activities brought in a declining percentage of their subsistence. All agree that few Ignacio Utes did much farming in the decade 1911-1921, but Hispanic share-tenants were working many allotments.

The transition in subsistence activities thus appears much less complete than the FRC records would indicate. In effect, the majority of Ignacio Utes became marginal rentiers, partly dependent on their own efforts at farming and stockraising but even more dependent upon the harvest shares they received from their Hispanic tenants, supplemented by income from leases and Government payments.

There are some apparent reasons for this transitional lag, of which perhaps the most fundamental is that settled life on ranches had few attractions for most Ignacio Utes, at least in the first fifty years of life on their reservation and, so long as alternative and supplementary means of subsistence were open to them they were unlikely to tackle farming in dead earnest. If Agent Weaver's remarks on the work patterns and attitudes he observed in 1877 are recalled, it is clear that successful southwestern irrigation farming would have required a total reorganization of Ute work habits. In a drought year, after all, many neighboring non-Ute ranchers lost their crops despite their efforts.

Vocational training at the Southern Ute Boarding School left something to be desired in promoting subsistence activities, in that Ute boys were given little training in anything but farm work, whereas many of them seem to have had aptitudes for other skills. The very fact that girls were given no outdoor farm training was out of line with traditional Ute involvement of women and children in food gathering and the care of livestock. It was also out of line with the many outdoor activities of Anglo and Hispanic neighbors, both children and women. Among both groups, child labor was prevalent and school attendance was frequently sketchy. The cooking, baking, laundry, and sewing skills taught to the Ute girls with school equipment could not be carried on in ill-equipped tents and brush shelters.

It must be noted, however, that some of the skills girls learned at the Southern Ute Boarding School did lead to marginal employment. Some, such as the Ute sisters named Shoshoni and other relatives, worked as domestic workers and hotel employees.[14]

Many of the boys demonstrated mechanical ability and, by 1911, enough young men could handle and repair tractors to inspire the suggestion that they be encouraged to buy their own farm machinery from their Individual Accounts.[13] Through school and work records of individual Utes run comments as to their ability in carpentry and Agency "engineer" tasks.

Two factors, however, reduced the use of learned skills in gainful employment. One was the limited number of skilled jobs open to Utes and the generally low rate of pay for the jobs which were available. Superintendent Werner commented in 1911 that a 10-hour day of labor in the beet-fields of Rocky Ford at $1.50 per day minus living costs provided less of a livelihood than the Ignacio Utes could make at home.[13]

The other factor was the reluctance of many Utes with marketable skills to accept steady jobs. "In last two winters I worked at the Agency and I would like to get a job there," wrote Julian Baker in 1917 when he wanted to make money to build a house. "I don't like to work in a engine room. Because if I work in engineer I got to stay with every day even if it is raining or snowing. But if I work outside then I don't have to go on rain or snowing days. . . . And I rather be working by the days instead by the month. . . . Because I have some stock to look after during the bad weather when I cant do anything outside."[15] In this instance, the objective of keeping a foot in each of two camps of partial subsistence is apparent.

Some measure of Ute reluctance to turn to wage labor for anything beyond a seasonal stopgap may have been due to the fact that, like many of their non-Ute ranching neighbors, the Utes liked to be their own bosses and not constantly subject to orders. Agent Weaver showed awareness of this fact in an 1877 exchange of letters on the desirability of having all his charges vaccinated. Said Weaver: "A simple request made to them will be more effective than a positive order."[16] Years later, it was stated that the best farmers among the Ignacio Utes were those living farthest from the Agency, never visited by Agency Farmers and never included in seed estimates.[17] Among these were the Utes and part-

Utes of the Animas and La Plata valleys and the Spencer-Baker kindred and Washingtons of the upper San Juan Valley. Some were doing their own work and some were employing Hispanic share-tenants, but all enjoyed the benefit of non-interference.

The Stimulation of Individual Enterprise

The *stimulation of individual enterprise* conducted by the Agency assumed different forms in different periods, according to changing circumstances and Indian Office policy. Carrot-and-club tactics were used in the main but it is doubtful how effective, in the long run, either tactic proved to be.

There were two obstacles throughout in the drive for individual enterprise. One was Ute lack of enthusiasm for farming, the principal vehicle of such enterprise. The other was the tendency to share the goods and moneys provided under the Treaties for implementing such enterprise far beyond the individuals for whom they were intended. Successive Agents over many years remarked on this traditional Ute method of redistributing resources, and found it annoying. Not that there seems to have been any rigid protocol on sharing but rather a collective enjoyment of anything that happened to be on hand, with no calculated husbanding of resources.

It was only in the years following the 1910 Judgment, proceeds of which were directly deposited in the Individual Indian Accounts of every man, woman, and child both of the Ignacio and Ute Mountain Utes, that the Utes finally were curbed in redistributing resources as they saw fit. In those same years, the total amount of the ration was drastically cut and the numbers receiving rations were reduced, as has already been shown in chapter 4. The only resource left for the Ignacio Utes to share was land. Since only a third of them owned allotments by 1921, this resource was scarce.

Reduction of the ration and its limitation, more or less, to minors and less able-bodied adults and also the initiation of the Reimbursable system were the main club tactics used to spur individual initiative. Following hard on a long period of handouts, they came as a great shock to the Ignacio Utes and provoked resentment.

In the years preceding allotment and for some years thereafter, the carrot tactic had been extensively used, largely to buy the goodwill of leading men, although the rationale was always that it was a reward for being industrious and setting a good example. Examples through the years of this tactic include the Gratuity payments from 1881 to 1890; the salaried status of Indian Police; the setting up of pre-allotment farms in the 1880s along with issues of farm implements and wagons to the "deserving, industrious Indians" whose share-tenants, by and large, worked the farms; the double allotments in 1895 to certain leading men and, by 1911, limited control over their own bank accounts and lease transactions for Ignacio Utes designated as "competent."

A highly favored group was thus created in the first quarter-century of Agency operation, having an income level much higher than most Utes and having much more access to opportunities for developing individual enterprise. Some of the favored Utes, such as Charles Buck, Severo, White Frost, and George Bent, did continue with relative success after special favors were withdrawn early in the twentieth century, but others did not. Close perusal of the names appearing with repetitive regularity among the "favored" of the early years shows that in some cases the recipients of favor were very far from demonstrating the type of initiative which was supposedly being stimulated. Mariano and Red Jacket, for instance, were for years on the Police and Gratuity payrolls, at the very time when their "energy and perseverance" were being dedicated to the "pursuit" of cowboys at the western end of the reservation. Quartro (Jacob Wing) was included on the same rolls for no better apparent reason than that he was the brother-in-law of Ignacio. Other names of less prominent men, recommended by the Agent for some specific achievement, were not included on the payrolls.[18]

It can fairly be concluded that the early policy of concentrating preferential treatment upon a limited segment of Utes was condemned from the start by its double objective. That it was a failure in the long run is demonstrated by the fact that from the totality of the favors listed no permanently affluent segment of Ignacio Utes emerged.

Later efforts to stimulate initiative were more rational and more successful. From 1907 on, a Southern Ute Fair was held most years, with exhibits of choice produce and stock, raised by the Ignacio Utes themselves and with cash prizes awarded which the Utes themselves raised by subscription. Utes were familiar with fairs and apparently took pride from the start in having one of their own. They also were successful in enlisting the support of local businessmen. Superintendents' reports on these fairs frequently expressed surprise at the excellent showing of the Utes and enthusiasm over the success of the enterprise.[19] Still, in 1925, Superintendent McKean had to explain to an Agency Farmer that his main task was to build ambition among Ute farmers and instill in each the "desire to surpass his fellows."[20]

The Acquisition of Private Property

The acquisition of private property, such as land allotments, permanent houses, farm equipment, and money in Individual Indian Bank Accounts presented the Ignacio Utes with forms of property which were new to them.

They also faced controls over the transfer of property, particularly as reflected in inheritance, which required a new set of adjustments. In the past, accumulation of property other than livestock was inhibited by roving existence, and goods were shared rather than saved. The new forms of private property were not all acquired at once. In fact, it was not until the 1895 Allotment that the Utes acquired a type of property which could not be handled in traditional non-accumulative ways.

Rations, annuity money, and livestock could be shared, consumed, or gambled away. Farm implements and seed could be passed on to the Hispanic tenant farmers for their use or could be sold. Agent Page described in 1880 the traditional disposition of property of a deceased Ute: "when one of their number dies, the tent or lodge of the deceased, with blankets, gun and other articles are at once burned, several of their best horses killed, and the entire band remove to some other locality."[21]

The allotment of land in severalty, under 25-year restricted patents, provided a form of property which the heirs of deceased Utes could not dispose of in traditional ways. Even before Allotment, Agent Day undertook to demonstrate to the Utes that no harm would come to them by remaining near the site of a death. When Karatch (Henry Clay) died in 1894 and his relatives hastily fled the premises saying the ground was "bewitched," Day set up an Agency farm there. He took out a fine crop, after which Karatch's relatives returned to the site and camped there.[22]

It appears possible, however, that the many cases of Ignacio allottees living on lands other than their own as late as 1913 had something to do with fear of remaining near the camps of recently deceased kin. In the years directly following allotment, many allottees died. The many years of delay in determining heirship may have had to do with reluctance of the next of kin to identify themselves and have to brave close association with the property of the dead.

There were further factors making for difficulty in determining heirs. The assigning of English names on the early annuity rolls was made in the profoundest ignorance of some very close kin ties, and assigning new names in later years only compounded the confusion. To an extent, the failure to establish names by kindred was the result of the laziness of Agency personnel, who only saw the Utes when they lined up to be paid and were only concerned to prevent double payments.

For years, the identification of nearest kin did not go much beyond the assigning of one surname to a mother and her minor children. On the other hand, when Agent Weaver, in early 1878, tried to get his charges to line up by family groups to receive their first annuities, they flatly refused and nobody would consent to give his name. No reason was given. Said Weaver: "Why these

Indians are so reluctant to make known their names I am not able to understand, neither can I ascertain the cause from those who have been acquainted with their habits and customs for the past fourteen years."[23] It is clear, therefore, that the Utes pursued an early policy of keeping Agency personnel in the dark as to their family identity. Apparently, it never occurred to the Agents to encourage their employees to visit at the Ute camps and become acquainted with Ute families to learn who was who.

Agency personnel repeatedly suggested that the Utes were a trifle hazy themselves as to their kin ties. While it does appear that Ute kin functions were relatively informal and flexible, there is evidence in the FRC records for much more kin recognition and function than recognized by the Agency personnel. For instance, adoption of minor orphans by "tribal custom" seems to have been universal and to have followed a regular procedure. An orphaned child was raised by a grandparent or by a sibling of one of the deceased parents. Lacking these, a more remote relative took the child, so that on the early Annuity rolls no homeless orphans were recorded.

Unfortunately, records were not kept as to the relationship between an orphan and the adopting relative. In 1897, Tom Sage was suspected of child desertion when it turned out that Carolina Chase, a minor "orphan" being raised by Tapuche (Nathan Price) was Sage's daughter. The fact is that Tom Sage was the son of Tapuche and had given the girl to her grandparents to raise after the death of his wife.[24]

Superintendent Werner in 1910 took note of "tribal custom" in adoptions when he urged that some siblings of the House family be declared heirs of Mary Jones, who had been raised by their mother, her distant relative. He proposed that all "tribal custom" adoptions prior to allotment be recognized as valid.[25] Had this proposal been adopted, the confused record of kinship in the Southern Ute Agency records could have been corrected. The discontinuity between original Ute names and the names arbitrarily assigned by Agency employees, including surname changes close to the turn of the century, when the tribal rolls were misplaced, could have been avoided.

We know, for instance, that Severo was the forefather of the Richards family; Buckskin Charley was the forefather of the Buck family; Ojo Colorado was the forefather of the Red family; Tapuche (also known as Nathan Price) was the forefather of the Sage family; Talian was the forefather of the Spencer family; Ankatash, an Uncompahgre leader, was baptized as Chico Velásquez in the San Luis Valley and acquired the Agency name of John Allen; his son, Cuatagá, was baptized as Felipe Velásquez and became James Allen. Karatch became Henry Clay. It seems likely that Aguila was the forefather of the Eagle family and Juan Anche was the forefather of the Thompson family. Other leading personages of the 1870s and 1880s are harder to track in later generations. Such are Cabezón, Ojo Blanco, Cabeza Blanca, Mariano, Juan Tobase, Padre (Spanish nicknames); also Senup, Shoshoni, Abiquiu, Peketagone, Carneritch, Passagouche, and other leaders mentioned in the early records.

Following allotment, heirship to the estates of deceased Ignacio Utes had to be determined under the laws of Colorado, and guardians of orphaned minors were appointed by the local courts. The FRC records contain scant correspondence on some of these cases and some transcripts of hearings held at the Agency in which Ute witnesses identified the relatives of deceased allottees as a preliminary to an heirship finding. These documents give a partial glimpse, suggestive rather than conclusive, into the adjustment of the Ignacio Utes to the possession of inheritable property, cash and real, after some years of experience.

There seems to have been a trend on the part of Ute witnesses to back the claimants to an estate beyond those whom Colorado law would have recognized. This trend was encouraged by the fact that allotted children in numerous cases predeceased their parents, so that when the parents in turn died they left several allotments, with potential heirs to them scattered through all three Ute jurisdictions. Then the effort to determine which of the claimants was properly related by Colorado law was made, with the Utes defining the relationships.

The difficulties of making proper identifications were multiplied by the variety of English surnames for members of a single lineage; by the frequent Agency practice of assigning to children the maternal rather than the paternal surname, even in some instances where the name of the father was known; and finally by the fact that the Utes addressed first cousins by sibling terms and, in instances where orphaned first cousins were raised by their parents, could easily have thought that they were true siblings.

The possibilities for these various sources of confusion are demonstrated in the Riley-Cook-Lock heirship hearings, in which Benjamin North and an aged former Ignacio enrollee, long since living in Utah, were the principal witnesses. Between them, they established that Stephen, Nathan, Elmira, Babe, and Josie Cook had all been full siblings of Thomas Riley and Alice Lock. Thomas and Hannah Riley, in turn, had been the parents of Benjamin North, Susan Wolfbear, Birdie, Sally and Jennie Riley and, finally, James Bush.

The possibility that Susan Wolfbear was the same person as Jennie Riley is indicated by the fact that the Utah elder said his son Jacob Star had been married to Jennie Riley, who later left him for Nicholas Eaton; whereas Benjamin North identified his sister Susan Wolfbear as the former wife of Jacob Star and current wife of Nicholas Eaton. It seems doubtful that two sisters would have been co-wives in sequence to two men, but the point was apparently missed in the hearing and Dick Eaton was later identified as the son of Susan Wolfbear's sister. It also appears possible that the uncharacteristically long list of two generations of siblings may have included some first cousins.

What is noteworthy about this is that distinctions of critical importance by Colorado law were of little functional significance in Ute tradition.[26] What is also noteworthy is that the confusion in the Agency records gave the Ignacio Utes opportunities to influence the selection of heirs.

The observable brittleness of the marriage relationship among the Utes seems to be reflected in some instances of challenges by blood kin of the deceased regarding the right of a surviving spouse to inherit, on the grounds that at the time of the death the marriage was inoperative.[27] Plurality of wives also created problems and disagreements. In 1913, Frank Howe was not supported by Ute witnesses in his claim to be the son of Talian (Job Spencer) by Polly Rice; in fact Talian's widow, Ida, said he was a nephew. In 1928, however, after all of Talian's offspring by Ida had died with the exception of Peter Spencer, the latter corroborated Howe's original claim.[28]

Tawache (Charles Adams) also claimed to be a son of Talian in 1913 but was induced to relinquish his claim. Hispanic informants who knew both Talian and Adams are of the opinion that Adams was Talian's son, but since Adams had been raised as a Hispanic "captive" and had been enrolled at Ute Mountain in 1900, there were no Southern Ute witnesses on his behalf.[29]

Plurality of wives and brittle marriage unions resulted in what must have appeared to the Utes to be injustice in the inheritance of estates of deceased offspring. By Colorado law, a living father was sole heir to such estates and the mother, if divorced, could not inherit from her own children until after his death, if at all. Daisy Spencer Baker became highly indignant when James Baker, to whom she had been co-wife in the 1890s along with her sister, Eliza, was declared heir to the estates of all his deceased children. She accused Baker of denying that he had ever been married to her and of trying to pass off some of her late children as the late Eliza's. When it was proposed that Baker deed to her a small part of the property that he was inheriting and that she in turn relinquish future claims as an heir to Baker's estate, she refused on the grounds that her living children would then lose their rights.[30]

Other than inheritance data, there is indication of another novel feature of ownership. This was the complete individualization of Indian Accounts in the name of every man, woman, and child of the three Ute jurisdictions to receive the proceeds of the Judgment Fund after 1911. These accounts, if reckoned by nuclear families, totaled a goodly sum in many instances, but withdrawals of any size required permission of the Indian Office, each request being mediated by the Superintendent. Such restrictions on cash outlays were a far cry from the free use, much less squandering, of annuity money. They also inhibited the pooling of resources, and caused hardships while Utes waited for the freeing of money from their own or their children's accounts.

Parents seem to have felt that their children's money was rightly theirs, as one such parent, trying to complete building of a home, expressed it to Superintendent McKean: "Send me my money, not yours (mine, mine)," she wrote irately in requesting speedy freeing of her children's accounts.[31]

Administrative emphasis on individual rather than joint ownership of the new forms of property, as well as Agency and Indian Office control over money beyond petty cash, may have served to promote loosening of kin ties especially in the years following the 1910 Judgment. Those were the years when per capita payments in the main were being deposited into Individual Indian Accounts, so that the only cash readily available was that earned through labor by individuals. Those were also the years of drastic reduction of food rations, especially beef.

It is not an illogical guess, therefore, to interpret as an indication of narrowing kin function and some decline in family closeness the following: rapid loosening of joint residence patterns between 1911 and 1913 and the end of Ute resistance to sending children to distant boarding schools as of 1913. In 1911, 362 Ignacio Utes were listed as comprising 52 families, of which 9 lived in tents. In 1913, 360 Ignacio Utes were listed as comprising 149 families of which 45 lived in tents. House-building was going on in these years but so, also, was dispersal into smaller family units.[13, 32]

The first group of Ignacio students to be sent away without protest from their parents since the 1885 fiasco at Albuquerque went to Santa Fe in 1913. There were 7 of them, out of a total of 94 "capable" school age children. In 1921, of a total of 102 "capable" Ignacio students, 17 were attending non-reservation boarding schools[5, 32] and by 1926 the number had apparently mounted.[33]

Political Change

Carl Schurz's 1877 program foresaw the day when individual Indians would voluntarily relinquish tribal relations and enter into the full status of American citizenship. For the Utes, superficially, there seemed to be no firm bar to such a transition, for they had no formal tribal structure in the first place. In fact, it is questionable to what extent the Ute bands were aboriginally distinct units. In the 1896 Council, Charles Buck hinted that the listed bands placed on reservations were a Government creation.[34] Some individuals shifted freely from band to band. Severo is supposed to have been a Muwach, but became a chief of the Kapotas. Leadership shifted, apparently dependent upon the persuasive powers of individuals and the size of their voluntary followings at different times.

An early and prolonged trend of Government relations with the Utes was the practice of kingmaking. Ignacio was officially recognized as the "head chief of the Southern Utes" and, while this selection was soon regretted, Ignacio's personal prestige among the Utes made it hard to "depose" him thereafter. But Tabewatch (Topoache on the 1885 Gratuity Roll) was deposed for having expressed approval of the Meeker "Massacre." He was described as a "war chief of influence" among the Kapotas, whereas Tapuche (Nathan Price) was their "hereditary chief." The Indian Office decided to "depose" both and make Severo chief spokesman for the Kapotas. Severo thus fell heir to Tabewatch's 1895 payment of $250, since Tabewatch had died.[35]

Despite such maneuvers, the Government was at no time able to produce a Southern Ute leader who would unreservedly support Government policy nor, for that matter, one who could command the support of all Southern Utes. The nearest approach to such a leader was the illustrious "Buckskin Charley," later renamed Charles Buck. His talent and "reasonableness" were immediately recognized and in 1880 the Hatch Commission proposed that he be named head chief in place of Ignacio.[36] Yet Charles Buck was by no means as tractable under official prodding nor yet as dominant among the Utes as the Government could desire. In the 1896 Council which voted to launch the first Claims case, Buck denounced the Government for duplicity, winding up with the classic phrase: "Washington heap liar all the time."[37]

In the post-allotment years, Buck was "chief" of the Ignacio Utes and continued in this honorary role until his death but Government blessings did not assure the tractability of his following. In 1917, the allegiance of the older Utes was said still to be with him, "but the younger men and women do not give him the same consideration."[38]

By 1920, whereas Buck was described as "helpful and in support of the local office," the tendency of many Utes to heed the encouragement of their Hispanic friends to "defy" the Superintendent was being deplored.[39] Apparently, by 1925-1926, Buck chose to repudiate the "local office" when the tribe elected him to head up the 1926 delegation to demand an accounting in Washington of past Judgment Fund expenditures.[40]

It appears, then, that neither the punitive pressures of which Ignacio was the main butt nor the preferential treatment accorded to Charles Buck and Severo created any serious change in the role of leadership among the Ignacio Utes. Leadership authority continued to rest on personal popularity and to be effective only to the extent that it voiced the consensus of opinion.

Apparatus for collective leadership did grow, however, with a new feature, the participation of women in the "tribal council" which, for some years preceding and following the establishment of the reservation, was composed solely of leading men to negotiate agreements with the U.S. Government. By

1888, all adult males were called upon to sign these agreements, which required by law a two-thirds favorable vote to be submitted to Congress. Participation in councils thus became more inclusive. Council meetings were infrequent, however, and their primary function was to endorse proposals initiated by the Government. The 1896 Council for launching the Claims case was the first such meeting on record to represent Ute interests in opposition to the Government. Agent Day attended the meeting but his remarks, if any, were not recorded and he appears not to have offered any objection to the decisions.[41]

For some years thereafter, there is no record of tribal council meetings of the Ignacio Utes, but in 1911 Superintendent Werner reported that the Tribal Council met twice a month to take up questions of estates and heirship as well as those of tribal welfare. Anyone who wished to attend was welcome.[13] The practice was continued through the West tenure. West also used the Council as an occasion for delivering homilies on the need for more application to farming.[42] His successor, Superintendent McKean, however, managed for years to veto Tribal Councils of Ignacio Utes, it being his opinion that "most of the efforts of these councils are misdirected and obtain for disorganizing and hindrances rather than for advancement."[43]

When the Consolidated Ute Agency was formed, McKean found it hard to cope with the 5-member Ute Mountain Tribal Council, which took decisions consistently contrary to the "wishes of the Government or any outside white man."[44] This Council had assumed a role of pressuring the Government on demands from the very start. In 1900, the main issue under discussion was failure to provide the Ute Mountain Utes with a promised water supply.[45] By 1905, a delegation to Washington was demanded to take up the issue of the failure to fulfill verbal promises made at the time of the 1895 Allotments.[46]

On March 21, 1926, the insurgent faction of Ignacio Utes called together a council which was attended by 52 Indians, including women and children. To McKean, who attended by invitation, the meeting was most distasteful, since a vote was taken to send a delegation to Washington to demand an accounting on the Judgment Fund, in which further criticism of "bureaucratic control" exercised by himself and the Indian Office would be voiced. McKean reported to the Indian Office that the meeting was not representative of Ute opinion, as demonstrated by the participation of women.[47]

The subsequent history of the Ignacio Tribal Council, as well as outspoken statements in the personal files on Ignacio Ute women, suggest, to the contrary, that this instance of feminine participation in tribal affairs was emblematic of an authentic new trend in collective leadership.

The Utes of southwestern Colorado, from the foundation of the reservation on the Pine River, showed a tendency toward factionalism, in which certain of their leaders formed loose alliances with outside forces for the attainment of limited goals. Ignacio's "wild" Wiminuches, by the summer of 1877, had already been discussing with local ranchers and businessmen where the Agency should be located.[48] The lengthy removal controversy was largely the product of local Anglo influence upon certain chiefs, mostly Wiminuches, possibly with the inducement of bribes. This is the only instance of any Ute-Anglo "alliance."

In the post-allotment years, those Ignacio Utes maintaining closest contact with the nearby Hispanic settlements were thereby encouraged to oppose Government policies and to direct their opposition into organized action. In this they had assistance from Hispanic friends and from certain Anglos closely associated with the Hispanos. Of all these, the most influential over the years were José Blas Lucero and Barry Sullivan.

Lucero, in the 1890s, set up a joint household with Paniuse (Henry Tree), called Panáyos by the Hispanos. The two became co-owners of a herd of sheep which they grazed near the La Plata Valley. Statements about him in the FRC records from 1897 to 1925 variously depict Lucero either as a total degenerate or as the best friend the Utes ever had, and the same range of opinion persists today. Living Utes who knew him best speak of him warmly.

In 1897, Lucero accompanied Henry Tree and Nathan Price on a delegation to Washington and the three conferred with the Secretary of the Interior, apparently regarding alleged irregularities at the Agency. In 1925 Lucero said that on this occasion the Secretary had instructed him to remain on the reservation as a watchdog over Ute interests, until certain records were placed in his hands. Lucero said that nobody had ever relieved him of this "trust."

Lucero and his kinsman, José Ignacio Lucero, accompanied James Allen, Joseph Spencer, Benjamin Tree, and John Ayers on the December 1925 delegation to Washington which launched the demand for an accounting of the Ute Judgment Fund and for the Ignacio Utes to have more control over their own affairs. While this delegation was denied official status, it was heard—resoundingly. Superintendent McKean countered the attacks upon his own conduct by rehashing every allegation made against Lucero since the 1890s.

Whether these allegations were true or not, the record shows that Lucero presented the Ute case with skill and boldness. Despite a probable lack of much formal education, he had a talent for litigation which is still legendary among the Hispanic population of the Ignacio area, especially those whose own ancestors were noted lay practitioners in the local Peace Courts.[49]

Lucero probably acquired much of his knowledge of the law from Barry Sullivan, with whom he was long associated. Sullivan was a prominent Durango attorney who for years had many Hispanic and Ute clients. He was cordially hated by the Agency leadership, starting in 1900. In that year, he inspired Steve Burch to exert his parental rights by removing his child from the Fort Lewis School, to which the child had been forcibly taken by the Indian Police.[50]

Sullivan also teamed with José Blas Lucero to instigate what was described as outright rebellion against the authority of Agent Smith, both at Ignacio and at Ute Mountain. Charles Buck served as a loyal informer to the Agent, but many of the Ignacio Utes were in the camp of Sullivan and Lucero.[51]

Whatever may have been the personal motives of Lucero and Sullivan, their long association with the Ignacio Utes left these Utes with confidence in their own capacity to seek redress of grievances and with some knowledge of procedural steps to attain these goals. While only a minority faction was in active alliance with Lucero and Sullivan, there seems to have been no counter-faction to the activities they promoted.

Changes in Education-Religion-Medicine

In the early reservation years, education of Ute children appears to have been entirely in the hands of their adult kin and to have been of a fairly informal nature. None of the early Agents took any note of specific training procedures nor, indeed, of anything except the fondly indulgent attitude of Ute parents toward their children.

There is no mention of the Dog Company, described by Opler as a military training society for young males.[52] Religious belief was neither dogmatic nor expressed by formal public ritual. Shamanistic practice for curing illness depended rather upon the supernaturally bestowed powers of the individual practitioner than upon a course of training. The Federal Records contain a description of the induction of shamans which does not contradict the main emphases of Opler's description of the buildup of shamanistic power.[53]

Statements made in this section, when not referenced by the FRC code, are based on interviews conducted with Ute, Hispanic, and Anglo informants in the years 1960-1962. While the first Agency reports state explicitly that no Ute had ever been to school, it seems altogether possible that those Utes who had been raised in Hispanic households had received some home training in reading and writing in Spanish and some indoctrination in the Catechism. The basis for this surmise is the differential tendency of these Utes and their offspring to welcome formal education, participate in the celebration of the Mass, and serve as godparents for newborn offspring as other Utes did not. Note particularly family data of Allen, Adams, Chavez, Head, Spencer, and Tree.[54]

More Utes than those raised in Hispanic households had some non-indigenous "education" from previous contact with Hispanos. Most understood some Spanish even if they could not speak it fluently, so that Spanish became a lingua franca of the Agency and the community. All seem to have had experience with the uses of money, including its application to such gambling games as Monte and "Koon Kan" (known as "Conquián" to the Hispanos) and the Indian hand game which the Hispanos called Cañute. No Utes spoke or understood English.

In 1883, 27 Ute children were sent to the Indian School at Albuquerque and, in 1885, 25 Ute girls were sent to the Convent of the Good Shepherd in Denver. While the group at Albuquerque made impressive progress in learning English, reading, and writing, the mortality rate was so high that in 1885 the grief-stricken and terrified parents demanded the return of all boarding school pupils and from that year until 1913 no substantial group of children was voluntarily sent to a distant school.[55]

In the intervening years, a certain number of Ute children were periodically forced to attend the Fort Lewis School near Hesperus in the La Plata Valley, which opened in 1892. A very few education-minded Ute parents occasionally allowed a promising child to be sent to Carlisle, Haskell, Grand Junction, or Santa Fe for further education.

The Utes were favorably disposed toward opening of a day school on the reservation. Such a school was inaugurated in 1886 and was attended by 12-14 out of 267 children of school age. Attendance dropped as soon as it was converted into a boarding school. In 1890, the school was closed.[56]

From 1890 to 1902, no Agency-operated school existed in the Ignacio area. In 1894, the Board of Presbyterian Missions supported the endeavor of Rev. A. J. Rodríguez to open a mission school near the Agency. Rodríguez had been invited to open the school by his friend and convert Julian Buck. In 1895, Agent Day reported that despite Rodríguez's praiseworthy efforts and Mrs. Rodríguez's free care for the sick, Catholic influence kept Ute attendance down.[57] In 1897, however, Day requested authority to pay Mrs. Rodríguez $25 per month, since Ute parents had expressed willingness to have her teach their children, and Day thought this might be an entering wedge to overcome the opposition which the Fort Lewis School controversy had by now solidified against all schools.

The Commissioner of Indian Affairs denied the request but said that if Mrs. Rodríguez would take a Civil Service examination she could operate a Government day school.[58] By 1900, the Rodríguez school had an Anglo teacher, instruction was in English only, and 37 Ignacio Ute children were enrolled, although average attendance was only 17.[59]

With the opening in 1902 of the Southern Ute Boarding School at the Agency, a new stage in the education of the Ignacio Ute children was launched. Being right on home grounds, it aroused no parental opposition and by 1904 its 60-student capacity was stretched to accommodate 70. In 1912, when all children who lived within walking distance attended the Allen Day School, operated by the Agency, the Boarding School still had 57 students. In addition,

Photo 7.1. Sunday School: Rev. A. J. Rodríguez, Severo, and Julian Buck
(J. E. Candelaria Collection, with permission)

by 1912, a handful of Ute children in the Animas and La Plata valleys were attending the public schools nearest them and two Utes were attending the Ignacio Public School.[12, 60]

By 1926, the Southern Ute Boarding School had been converted into a boarding school for Navajo students. The Consolidated Ute Agency listed 250 children of school age, of whom 38 were rated "ineligible" for school. Eighty-six were attending the boarding school at Ute Mountain, 39 were away at non-reservation boarding schools, 37 were in public schools, 22 attended the Allen Day School, and 36 "eligibles," living in the Allen Canyon-Blanding area, were attending no school. The preponderant influence in the training of youth had clearly passed from the hands of kin groups and was now centered in schools.

From the earliest school reports on through the years, educators made favorable mention of the learning ability and eagerness of Ute students. Early good performance may have been partly due to careful selection of students, to a preponderance of pupils from "favored" families, to some previous learning in Spanish, or to a combination of these factors. Generally good performance in learning continued to be observed of Ignacio Ute students, but also discipline problems due to pride and sensitive feelings.

At Albuquerque, David Root was reported to have become "swell-headed" because of his recognized skill in carpentry. When reproved for being pert to a woman teacher, he ran away from school.[61] Through the Fort Lewis School years and thereafter, runaway Ute students were no rarity. They took refuge with friends and relatives, and their parents sided with them against the school authorities. In 1918, the transfer of Guy Mills from his post as Principal of the Southern Ute Boarding School was recommended, because his use of corporal punishment had offended the children and incensed their parents.[62]

Despite the years of school experience and the verdict of educators that the children were "bright," progress in literacy and English speaking was painfully slow among the Ignacio Utes, possibly because of high mortality among the students as well as among their parents. In 1905, out of an estimated Ignacio Ute population of 385, 75 were listed as English-speaking and 12 as literate. In 1911, out of a population of 362, there were 102 English-speakers and 57 literates. In 1921, the population was 329, the English speakers were 95 and the literates were 60.

In Ute tradition, there was no dichotomy between religious outlook and medical practice, both deriving from the same interpretation of natural phenomena as controlled by supernatural forces. No body of dogma prevailed in this interpretation, so that the Utes felt free to adopt new religious-medical practices without dropping their primary beliefs.

Organized missionizing was initiated with the opening of the Presbyterian School in 1894, paradoxically, in view of the fact that most of the Hispanic population and some Ignacio Utes were practicing Catholics. The few Catholic churches scattered through the area, however, were administered by circuit priests who conducted Mass at best once a month. Priestly activities among the Utes were minimal. In 1906, Rev. Duffy of Saint Columba Church in Durango reported to Superintendent Leonard, regarding his work among the Utes of a few years past, that he had conducted no marriage services. When baptizing some couples married by Indian Custom, he had had them repeat Catholic marriage vows. Rev. Duffy added: "Prior to my administration a Rev. Francisco Aguirre Muñoz visited Ignacio on one or two occasions and baptized a number of Indians. Quite possibly he may have had a ceremony of renewal of promises on these occasions. As no record was left by him I would infer that no regular marriages took place before him on these visits."[63]

Aside from infrequent visits by priests, a contributing factor to the minimal Catholic affiliation of most Utes who were nominally of that faith was the lack of missionizing zeal of their Hispanic neighbors. Between 1900 and 1920, the José Velásquez and Cornelio Valdez families served as baptismal godparents for the majority of Utes brought to the font at Ignacio. The preponderance of those baptized were elderly people, so that the godparent role did not carry the continuing responsibility that it did for the young. By contrast, in La Posta, the Ute and part-Ute children were baptized at an appropriately early age, due to the integrated situation in the community. They attended Mass, confessed their sins, and received the Sacraments.

By 1911, Superintendent Werner, in a drive to stabilize Ute marriages, "compelled" his charges to undergo a marriage ceremony by barring their children from the rolls until the marriage was formalized. In this drive, he found the Catholic Church a "help."[13] Yet such compulsion did not noticeably intensify Catholic observance among most Utes. Rev. I. Llevat of the Theatine Order wrote wistfully of the situation in 1917: "You know how difficult it is to find out those thinks from the Indian people. You know, my dear Mr. McKean, that a priest is not satisfied with the mere attendance to the Mass, he is obliged to do his best to lead them to the reception of the Sacraments."[64] At that time, 80% of Ignacio enrollees were listed as Catholics.[65] The impact of the Presbyterians and other Protestant sects had been of minimal proselytizing effect.

With the exception of that section of the Utes whose Catholicism was demonstrated in overt formal practice, the Ignacio Utes accepted affiliation with any church as something to be added on to traditional belief and practice. This pluralism of outlook was unacceptable to their Hispanic neighbors, who still find it paradoxical to see Sun Dancers wearing crucifixes.

The Utes accepted medical services as soon as they were offered, from smallpox vaccination to emergency surgery. When an Agency Physician was installed in 1881, they began coming in for treatment of ailments great and small. On the other hand, the services of shamans were likewise used without noticeable abatement for years. In 1891, Page Joy was brought to the Agency Physician a few days before his death, attributed to bronchitis and exhaustion from the "incessant din" of the shamans who had attended his bedside.[66] Agency Physicians, in one report after another, prematurely hailed the demise of shamanistic medicine, which declined after allotment of the Ignacio Utes but did not disappear until the 1960s.

The most conservative element with regard to medical treatment was comprised of the women. When venereal diseases were first detected in the late 1880s, men patients accepted treatment, at least until the primary symptoms disappeared, but not so the women. They were described as "mean and stubborn," some declaring that "they had rather die than be treated."[67]

Bodily modesty may account in part for the reluctance of the women to accept treatment for genitourinary conditions, but a stronger motive appears to have been the persistence of their traditional isolation during menstruation and childbirth. Few indeed were the births attended by Agency Physicians in the early days. The ratio of children continued small in relation to total population with a low birthrate recorded, due in part, it can be assumed, to the practice of allowing to die of exposure any child born with an observable defect.

One of the few births attended by an Agency Physician before the twentieth century was that of a child born with double harelip and cleft palate in 1892. The Physician reported: "The child died during the night from the effects of exposure I presume as the Indians never rear deformed children."[68] In 1894, Ute children were described by Agent Day as healthy, cheerful and "all perfect in symmetry as a Ute parent will not raise a child that is in any way deformed."[69]

The turnover rate in shamans was high in the early reservation years. Since the death of a patient was generally interpreted as due to the practice of "bad medicine" by the attending shaman, a revenge killing frequently ensued. In fact, most killings among the Utes in the early years were explained as motivated by revenge for supernatural harm inflicted on a victim by a practitioner of "bad medicine." Most were set down in the FRC records as "justifiable" and were not punished.[70]

In 1891, Nannice (George Norris) killed the shaman Chovita (Francis Carter), under whose care his son had died.[71] A later and more sensational revenge killing was that of Wap (Jacob Buffalo) after the death of a patient who was not only his own nephew but also the son-in-law of Ignacio. This happened in 1904 and, in an informal report, it was stated that the killing was considered justified by most Utes; furthermore, that such killings were generally kept secret among the Utes and were actually much more frequent than officially recognized.[72]

After allotment, reliance on modern medicine made far more rapid strides among the Ignacio Utes than at Ute Mountain. By 1916, it was announced that infant mortality at Ignacio had been cut 50% through a vigorous program of home visits by the field matron and the offer of prizes to the mothers of the healthiest and cleanest babies.

It was also announced that the Ignacio Utes were willing to have tribal funds used to build an Agency hospital, since they were "more than anxious to avail themselves of hospital treatment when ill."[42] In 1917, "there are still some old medicine men upon the reservation but their practices are practically dead and most of the Indians call for the white physician in all cases of sickness. I believe that each year these Indians are growing to appreciate more fully the services of the physician."[38]

Considering the high mortality rate among shamans recorded for the early years of Agency operation, along with early and widespread acceptance of mainstream medical care, the above statement is no doubt accurate in the main. Yet there are reasons for doubting that by 1926 shamanistic ideas about illness had disappeared among the Ignacio Utes even if shamanistic practices had declined.

Persistence of Ute religious outlook embodied in the spring Bear Dance as well as in the borrowed Sun Dance, coupled with Ute Mountain continuing shamanistic practice reinforced traditional views on health-illness. Certain Hispanic ideas regarding witchcraft that paralleled the Ute idea of "bad medicine" were still current. The emergence of the Native American Religion among the Utes at the turn of the century, marked by the use of peyote as medicine for the spirit, had reinvigorated indigenous thinking about the relationship between religion and medicine.[73]

A case of possible infanticide among the Ute Mountain Utes in 1925 shows the persistent influence of shamans there, and it is hard to believe that this influence did not extend somewhat to the Ignacio Utes through the steady contact they maintained with their Ute Mountain kin and friends. In this instance, a baby was born to the wife of Platt May in the camp of her father, Mormon Joe, described as a "medicine man of the old type."

Mother and child were buried together after the mother's death, Platt May declaring that the baby was still alive at the time of burial. Mormon Joe testified that the baby was born feeble, had not nursed and "had no hair." It had died the evening before burial. When the baby's body was exhumed, it was found to have a medicine bag tied about its neck. Mormon Joe said he had not placed the bag there and denied being a shaman, but Platt May contradicted him. He added that he did not fear death at the hands of his father-in-law, "but in a dream he would kill someone else."[74]

Chapter 8
Conclusion

Types of Culture Change

From the preceding sections, it is clear that not all categories of change were accomplished by the same means. The dynamics of change were quite complex and variable from 1877 to 1926. Even among the small segment of Ignacio Utes following the 1895 Allotment, always numbering less than 400, the degree of complexity and variability is notable. Another key factor is the relatively weak influence for change exerted by the Agency, despite its official control over livelihood and education. Below is a listing of the types of change noted, with illustrative examples.

Assimilative

A small percentage of Ignacio Utes, particularly in the area from La Posta to the La Plata valley and, to a lesser extent, in the immediate vicinity of Ignacio, showed a marked assimilative trend toward Hispanic ways, in family, religious, and social life, but to a much lesser extent in economic life and relations, and not at all in such forms of political participation as voting in general elections.

Most Utes of Southwestern Colorado, through previous contact with Hispanic communities, already had assimilated an understanding of the uses of money as a primary medium of exchange by the time the reservation was founded. Their determination to be paid the sums promised them in treaties and agreements with the U.S. Government was early and frequently expressed. After the 1895 Allotment, friends acquired by the Ignacio Utes through their close association with the Hispanic community, especially the team of Sullivan and Lucero, became a ready source of advice as to their rights and the procedures they should follow to secure them. They readily adjusted to the use of lawyers, and the individual files of Ignacio Utes show that an understanding of litigation procedures extended also into the personal field.

The only assimilative changes accomplished directly under the Agency program were the acceptance of Agency physicians and adoption of formal schooling for the children, which greatly altered socialization patterns, technological training, and language usage. Here, however, partial rejection on the part of the Utes becomes evident. The rejection was not of education itself, but of certain conditions and results associated with education.

The principal objection to schooling from the first years of the reservation to 1913, reinforced by the mortality figures among the first boarding school students, was to sending children away from home. This objection was motivated by parental affection and, probably to an equal extent, by fear of "bad medicine." Such fear could in no way have been assuaged by the practice of sending children home *after* they had become seriously ill.[1]

As more students attended school with regularity, sources of discontent among them became apparent. Anglo-style disciplinary procedures were resented, also the use as factotums of older students who were willing workers, without regard for the educational purpose of their boarding school attendance.[2] Three-year contracts for education at distant boarding schools cut down on home visits.[3]

Disillusionment that education could lead to a better life seems to have come from the corrupting aimlessness of the reservation life which awaited returned students. Here is how the matter was put by Superintendent Runke in 1914: "We are not especially proud of the young Indian men who have attended and passed school age at this Agency." Their school training, said Runke, had given them an appreciation of the "value of the comforts of civilization" but, through exposure to the "considerable element of inferior Mexicans and some few low down whites," they had learned such vices as excessive drinking, which the "older and more ignorant generation never learned."[4]

Syncretic

Old Meaning Recast in New Form

Mobility was to the Utes a way of life, built into their traditional economy which, as has been shown, became gradually inoperative under Agency conditions. Yet mobility was to a great extent maintained by extended visits to relatives and friends and participation in fairs and Wild West shows.

Another new form which became a vehicle for the expression of old meanings was the habitual sharing of the new means of subsistence obtained through Government agencies. Such sharing was curtailed by the drastic reduction in rations issued after 1911, along with deposit of most per capita payments into Individual Indian Accounts under control of the Agency and Indian Office. Utes continue to value the idea of sharing resources even though it has become much more difficult.

Mosaic (New Form with Innovations)

The principal adjustment of the Ignacio Utes to the ranching economy imposed upon them was a special development of the shares system of their Hispanic neighbors. The system was used without the growth of the patrón-peón relationship of the lower Rio Grande Hispanic communities. The Utes remained marginal owners, often no better off economically than the laborers who worked for them. The Hispanic share-tenants in the same years owned or were acquiring land and livestock of their own. Share agreements, "contracting" to provide share farmers and leasing of allotments, became an important factor in the local economy of non-Utes while the Ignacio Utes themselves lived on the fringes of local economic life.

Compartmentalized (Pluralistic)

In various categories, the partial acceptance of new forms without relinquishing old ones was characteristic of the adjustment of the Ignacio Utes. It seems, in fact, to have been their most characteristic tendency, reflecting, perhaps, the absorptive capacities of an underlying simple and flexible culture. Ranching, especially in its guise of providing minimal income by renting out lands, was adopted to a minimum required by necessity, while hunting and food-gathering were continued as much as conditions permitted. The total mixed and half-functioning economy was supplemented by money and goods received from the Government. Again, in the medico-religious field, the adjustment of the majority of Ignacio Utes over many years was to accept new forms in minimal fashion, while maintaining traditional values.

Results

By 1926, the following seems best to characterize the trends of change among the Ignacio Utes after fifty years of reservation life:

1) They had neither merged with nor become dominated by any segment of the forces composing contact relations, although a small sector in closest association with Hispanic Americans had voluntarily assimilated a number of features of Southwestern Hispanic rural culture. For most, however, identity as Utes and, in a broader conceptual sphere, as Indians, had been reinforced by the special conditions of their existence, including the benefits of their separate identity.

This point was eloquently voiced during World War I, in a statement opposing the registration of draft-age Ute men. After forty years of government insistence that the Utes become "civilized" by ceasing to be hunters and warriors, Ute youth was being recruited to a much deadlier form of carnage than anything the Utes had ever known. Old Pawishawa (John Weaselskin or William) had his young grandson Hickey William write down the following oration, in a translation to fractured English which nonetheless caught the vibrant spirit of the original:

> I am write to you now. What you think it now. What you think it me this my letter about this I talk to you now. And what kind man you are. This I gread know it we are Mr. Ouray son. I am his son we are. I am gread man of first man of this United States. But I am put away in earth gun. But we cant not war, no war. But I dont like this war. I dont like it that red river. But I like white earth, white land. How we Indian get our gun. Because this gun in earth. How, how took out. But all American are my brother and father and my cousin and my grandchildren and my good people too. All everybody are my son and brother all over the country. I kind to them I am. This is my talk, no, no war. And American woman and girl too and my sister and grandchildren and my mother no war, no war. I am Ouray Indian chief. We are kind to everybody. I dont like that war to my friend. But we have sheep, Washington sheep and everything we have. How we going keep when you talk like that. We are very old. Very old. If you dont believe come to see us. We are gread know. But just American and Mexican going to war not Indian.[5]

2) Rather than effecting sweeping changes, involving replacement of one way of life by another, the trend of change appears to have been limited and partial, due to Ute resistance to pressures and the fact that the Ignacio Utes had more alternatives than were officially offered.

3) There was a high degree of variability and complexity in the adjustments made by the Ignacio Utes, notable for such a small and closely linked population. To an extent, this was fostered by certain inconsistencies in Indian Office policy and Agency administration. For instance, programs aimed at economic self-support and an "industrious" way of life were contradicted by the annuities, rations, and paternalism which cultivated dependence. The giving or withholding of these benefits according to policy modifications or individual judgments only made for greater inconsistency. Charles Buck, for instance, was for years the recipient of special favors due to his influence in securing Ute acceptance of many Government measures. Yet in 1908 he was suddenly notified that the Government would not pay for a horse to replace one he had lost, since the "Government has stopped giving presents."[6] Again, in 1921, the Indian Office weighed the coercive effect of refusing young James Root the right to spend $300 from his bank

account to purchase sheep. The boy was supposed to be in school, yet his blind mother and grandmother had to be supported somehow and there were younger siblings in school. The father felt that family needs required that James herd sheep. "Tom Root, the father, has been to school and speaks fair English. He is therefore aware of the disadvantage under which his son will always labor if he is deprived of an education." The question remained, if the money was withheld until the boy went to school, would the father capitulate?[7]

The Government and its Agents were referred to, by Utes and Government personnel alike, in paternalistic terms, but in the Ute view, here was a bossy and stingy father indeed. John Kuebler, through his lawyer, made the following statement in a notarized complaint, charging Captain Abbot with having brought illness on his family by refusing to free Kuebler family bank accounts for completion of a home and, furthermore, causing his younger brother Fritz to be sent to jail in Denver on a liquor introduction charge, for lack of bail money from the same accounts: "Said agent's manner is overbearing and repulsive to affiant's people . . . he will not aid them when they are in trouble and will not listen to any of their complaints . . . he is not in sympathy with them and does not try to understand them." John Kuebler was joined in his demand that Abbot be removed from the Superintendency by his father Alphonso Kuebler and by Gus William, Burchard Hayes, and James Bush.[8]

Constant prodding in favor of individual initiative at the expense of sharing of resources produced variable reactions. Since none of the Agency programs did, nor in fact could, produce general prosperity among the Ignacio Utes, the tendency to share resources persisted wherever it could. For instance, Benjamin North, described as a "very good and peaceable Indian," was an Ignacio allottee living at Navajo Springs in 1913. He had a herd of several hundred sheep under the care of a paid herder, and his allotment was farmed on shares, until a Ute friend settled on it. Then North said he no longer wanted the allotment to be leased to a white man: "Alright Ute sit down all the time on it." The possible reciprocal benefit of such hospitality was lost on the Superintendent, who forthwith demanded that North return to Ignacio and live on his own land.[9]

Another point on which administrative inconsistency led to variable responses on the part of the Ignacio Utes was the question of the "citizen" status of allottees. It had been said that acceptance of allotment in severalty would make citizens of the Ignacio Utes and, so far as probate and heirship proceedings were concerned, the Government affirmed this status. Charles Buck was simply repeating what he had been told when he stated before the 1896 Tribal Council: "I am a white man, I am a citizen, and we are all citizens, all Americans."[10]

The restricted patents to allotments were supposed to terminate in 1921 and, from then on, the Utes were supposed to have unconditional rights over their property. Yet in 1918, while the Utes were being urged to affirm their citizenship by buying Liberty Bonds and their young men were being registered for possible Army service, the Commissioner of Indian Affairs cautiously explained that citizenship for the Ignacio Utes was an individual matter and must be decided on the facts of each case.[11] And in 1926, the Commissioner of Indian Affairs wrote to Edwin Taylor and James Baker: "It is true that all the Indians are now citizens, but this does not give them unrestricted control of their trust property nor affect the right and duty of the United States to administer such property for their best interests as required by various acts of Congress and departmental regulations in conformity therewith."[12]

Low social status and limited opportunity reinforced the conditions of wardship. Few Utes had clear ideas about their rights or tried systematically to exercise them. Those who were outspoken and insistent were scarcely popular at the Agency. When Mary Baker Peña complained to the Indian Office regarding Superintendent McKean's conduct, McKean retorted that she was "one of the educated Utes at this jurisdiction . . . she is the type of Indian who continually wants something." He added that she was a sister of Joseph Spencer who had been on the Washington delegation with José Blas Lucero, and concluded heatedly: "The tone of her letter is very misleading as well as ungrateful."[13]

4)   The final and most notable trend produced by fifty years of Agency life for the Ignacio Utes was the pervasive influence of their Hispanic neighbors, expressed in various ways and in many degrees of variability. The significance of this trend is heightened by nearly constant official discouragement from the Agency, although it appears that in private some Agency leaders encouraged the growth of systematic contact between the Hispanos and the Utes, especially in the field of mutual economic arrangements.

A much more powerful factor underlying this influence, however, was the fact that the Utes came on the reservation after nearly two centuries of frequent contact with Hispanic communities of northern New Mexico, during which they had made free, selective borrowings from Hispanic culture without being dominated or being obliged to give up their own culture. Fifty years of reservation life in close contact with Hispanic neighbors deepened the relationship under conditions of compatibility, mutual interest and, occasionally, common cause. It is also fair to state that the Utes, over the centuries, influenced their Hispanic neighbors at least as much as they were influenced.

Above all, and to their great credit, the Southern Utes managed not only to survive the ordeal of a half century of government coercion but to preserve the vital core of their own identity.

Afterword by Richard O. Clemmer:
Southern Ute Land, Economy, Culture, and Strategy under the Reorganization, Termination, and Self-Determination Eras

In order to understand Southern Ute strategy in the latter half of the twentieth century, some review of the devastating impacts of the allotment and assimilation policies is necessary. This review will establish the baseline from which Utes had to reconstruct much of their political economic identity as a Tribe. Therefore, we begin with a recapitulation of the allotment-assimilationist era.

Allotment

The severest test of Southern Utes' personal resilience and collective tenacity for persistence came with the allotment era. Allotment was a product of an assimilationist ideology. The intent of Congress during the last quarter of the nineteenth century was to turn "hostile" Indians into "friendly" ones and to integrate Indians into "the national life as independent citizens, so that they may take their places as integral elements in our society, not as American Indians but as Americans, or rather men, enjoying all the privileges and sharing the burdens of American citizenship."[1] Inauguration of Ulysses S. Grant's first administration in 1869 brought an effort to streamline the administration of Indian affairs and to apply a uniform policy to all reservations. Grant's second administration (1873-1877) saw successful lobbying on the part of Protestant churches engaged in missionary work; human rights advocacy groups such as the Indian Rights Association, formed entirely by non-Indians but which later included Indians who had become U.S. citizens; and the liberal wing of the Republican Party to influence Indian affairs.

The result was a uniform policy implemented on every reservation. Its intentions were to de-Indianize the Indians: that is, to make them into rural farmers of Christian faith, literate in English, skilled in blue-collar professionsthat would turn Indian communities into approximations of rural American towns, unfettered by ancient traditions and customs. Its cornerstones were:

1) day schools (later boarding schools) staffed with teachers
2) one or more resident missionaries
3) a resident agent (special agents were employed where residencies were not established)
4) one or more resident or visiting technicians, usually farmer or mechanic or both
5) a resident physician

The purpose of such a staff was to administer the Reservation so that its inhabitants would eventually become either rural yeoman or rural proletariat, differing only in the color of their skin and knowledge of their heritage from surrounding populations of American homesteaders. The policy took no account of the diversity of lifestyles, cultural heritage, or economies of American Indian communities, nor did it accommodate the possibility that, if given a choice, many American Indians would have preferred to remain who they were.

To these ends, agents were authorized to form squads of all-Indian police; to set up either courts of Indian offenses or Tribal courts; and to designate one or more "chiefs" or "captains" as both the Indians' official representative to the agent, and the agent's de jure appointee in keeping the lid on dissent and unrest. The agent also set up a Court of Indian Offenses, usually with a non-Indian chief judge and one or more Indian associate judges. Thus reservations became not just places, but also distinct and separate administrative units of the U.S. Government. Agents set up systems of distribution, loan, or sale of farming implements to Indians; outlets for marketing of crops; and freighting contracts in which Indians were encouraged to purchase wagons for a modest down-payment, and then were paid to haul freight for the BIA and crops for reservation farmers. On the Southern Ute Reservation, Severo—a former Muache chief—was made "Captain" of the agency-controlled Southern Ute police.

Between 1870 and 1910, local interests made continual efforts to abolish the Southern Ute reservation and either to allot all reservation lands to Indians in severalty with no restrictions on alienation of the allotments, or to have the Indians moved to the Uintah and Ouray reservation in Utah.[2] In 1887, Congress passed the Dawes Allotment Act. The Dawes Act and its subsequent amendments partially pacified these local interests with regard to the lush lands of the Southern Utes but also represented something of a compromise since it did place restrictions on the alienation of allotments and ostensibly provided irrigation water and technical assistance in farming to the Indians. Allotments could not be patented to individuals, and thus could not be sold ("alienated") for a period of 25 years after being allotted.

Following passage of the Dawes Act, three specific goals drove the BIA's program:

1) dividing collectively held tribal land into privately owned, individual family allotments of 640 acres or less and confiscating remaining lands for distribution to U.S. citizens
2) suppressing Indian religious ceremonies and social dances that missionaries found offensive and, after 1892 when Congress made education compulsory for Indians
3) schooling in boarding institutions

Education was probably the most important component of the allotment policy. Education was crucial to implementing the policy's general goals to "relieve the government of the enormous burden" of operating the reservations, and also to "settle the Indian question within the space generally allotted to a generation." By forcing children to attend school, the Indian Office sought not only to enhance literacy but also to "civilize" the "natives" by removing them from tribal influences and to stamp out Indian languages by forbidding children to speak anything but English under threat of corporal punishment. Vocational courses of study with emphasis on agriculture, technological skills, and homemaking would integrate Indians into the rural proletariat.[3] The BIA developed the tradition of reservation boarding schools during this period. Before 1890, the Bureau had sent a few Utes to the Good Shepherd Boarding School in Denver and to the Colorado Industrial School in Grand Junction, under contract. But beginning in the 1890s, the Bureau began building boarding schools directly on the reservations and eliminated contract arrangements.

The ideology that framed this program justified it in the following terms: The experience of handling private property would promote knowledge of how to handle it; encourage entrepreneurship; promote the ethical values of nascent capitalism and wage labor; and shift the concept of responsibility from tribe and community to the individual, thereby heightening awareness of the obligations of individualized citizenship. Isolating children in boarding schools away from the "barbaric" influences of parents and community would result in the quick breakup of Indian societies. Suppressing Indian religion would ease missionaries' efforts to replace Indian beliefs and moral codes with Christian ones. The ideology rested on the false assumptions that Indians would naturally want to be like Anglo-Americans; that tribal ties, conducive to lack of competitiveness for upward social mobility, were doomed; and that Indians could not succeed economically without shedding most of their culture.

Indians at this time were not in a position to participate in developing policies affecting them. No system of representation of Indians in the U.S. Government existed. Indians were not citizens. They had been purposely isolated from U.S. citizens by Government policy. Until 1871 they had been treated as citizens of separate, sovereign, "domestically dependent" nations,[4] with all of the liabilities of small foreign nations surrounded by a much larger and more powerful one, and few of the privileges. But under the assimilation/allotment policy, each Indian reservation became merely a "small department of the federal Government"[5] and even the pretenses of domestic dependent sovereignty were abandoned.

The allotment period was preceded by desultory attempts on the part of agents to get Utes to farm. Southern Utes had had little experience in farming; they liked to do hunting, gathering, and trading and were best at it. Only when occasional opportunities arose did they turn to farming. The Los Pinos agent reported in the 1880s that 30 Indians farmed 75 acres and sold part of the produce to U.S. troops and other Whites. Although the Capote, Muache, and Weeminuche (Witapinuche) had developed small herds of sheep, goats, horses, and cattle, the Southern Ute agent reported in 1880 that "none of these Indians make any attempt at farming; they refuse all offers of schools; none speak English; a greater portion understand some Spanish. . . . They live in tents or brush lodges, and frequently move from one portion of the reservation to another."[6] By 1890, the agent reported 600 acres in cultivation under oats, wheat, barley, corn, melons, squash, pumpkins, and potatoes. Fourteen children were attending a small day school.[7]

However, nearly half the Southern Utes had virtually no experience with farming. By 1885 nearly all the Weeminuche (Witapinuche) had gone west of the La Plata Mountains under the leadership of Chief Ignacio to the unirrigated, more barren, western portion of the 1.2 million acre reservation. From there, the Weeminuche frequently ranged into eastern Utah.

In 1895 the Utes who had remained along the Las Animas, Florida, Los Pinos, and Piedra Rivers were pressured to accept an agreement to take allotments and to cede 95% of the remaining land to the U.S. Government for homesteading by its citizens. Thus, allotment began and the reservation was prepared for Anglo homesteaders. Construction was begun on an extensive system of irrigation ditches, and Southern Utes were expected to become yeoman farmers. But most of the irrigation water ended up going to non-Indian homesteaders who took most of the best lands. Homesteaders took all but about 30,000 acres of the best lands and some Indian allotments were sold off by the agent around 1925 ostensibly on behalf of Indians that he had deemed "incompetent." Southern Utes who did take allotments were allowed to retain some communally held Tribal land, and by 1900, Southern Utes on the allotted portion of the Reservation had 2,600 sheep; 1,000 goats; and 85 cattle. They raised 3,000 tons of wheat; 350 tons of hay; and 8,500 tons of oats, barley, and rye.[8] By 1905, 375 allotments had been made, but only 40 Indians were living on them; most preferred to remain in extended family living situations, letting their allotments stand idle or hiring Hispanic farmers to improve and farm the allotment for a share of the crop.

Although continuing to camp along the La Plata River, the Weeminuche under Ignacio refused farming allotments between 1895 and 1910, and although Ignacio did not, most of the Weeminuche as well a some Capotes and Muache retreated permanently to the unirrigated portion of the reservation. By 1915, band affiliation and leadership had been submerged under a government-inspired dichotomy: Utes who farmed, and those who did not farm. The non-farmers west of the La Platas eventually became known as the Ute Mountain band and eked out a living on a barren 525,000 acres by sheepherding, hunting, gathering, government rations, and trading some craft items to Navajos. The Southern Utes lived east of the La Platas by farming, sheepherding, hunting, and government rations. By 1915 their land had become restricted to less than 40,000 acres.

The severe population decline that affected American Indians generally also prevailed among the Southern Utes. By 1920, the population had sunk to an all-time low of 334 under the jurisdiction of the Ignacio agency and 462 Mountain and White Mesa Utes under the Towaoc and Allen Canyon agencies. Southern Ute ditches, built nearly entirely with Indian labor, were largely in service to Anglos, and agriculture on the Southern Ute Reservation was largely also in the hands of Anglos. Share-farming arrangements that benefited both the Ute owners of allotments and the Hispanic farmers who farmed them were discouraged or banned completely. Economically, Utes came to approximate peasants: truck gardens, chickens, and some sheep and goats provided subsistence resources, supplemented by hunting, with occasional surpluses being traded to the agent in return for scrip which could be used to purchase commercial items such as coffee and sugar at local stores and trading posts. The agency distributed treaty annuities in the form of rations of meat and sometimes flour, weekly or biweekly. A lawsuit filed in the U.S. Court of Claims in 1909 resulted in a three-million-dollar judgment for lands taken from Utes of Colorado. But these funds were placed in a bank account and could be drawn upon only in small amounts with the written permission of the agent until the 1940s. Most of the time, individuals were issued scrip which was redeemable at Hans Aspaas's store; Aspaas would then be paid in cash by the agent from the individual's account.

By 1911, Buckskin Charley had emerged as undisputed Chief of the Southern Utes at Ignacio. Buckskin Charley had come to prominence in 1886 as the young, vigorous leader of the Capote band. He seems to have acquired the position by attempting to shape U.S. policy with regard to the Southern Utes, joining Ignacio and Tapuche in airing grievances and making specific requests to the Commissioner of Indian Affairs on a visit to Washington, D.C. Throughout the first decades of the twentieth century, Charley continued to support the adoption of particular Hispanic families and selected non-Hispanic individuals by Ute families.[9] He supported the growth and institutionalization of the Sun Dance, and despite official disapproval of the BIA between 1905 and 1933,[10] the Sun Dance became the major form of Ute religious expression.[11] Peyotism also made its appearance at this time and Emma Buck—Charley's wife—was one of its major proponents and Charley became Ignacio's first road chief, unbeknownst to agency personnel who disapproved of it heartily and denied its existence among the Utes.[12]

Perhaps Peyotism went undetected because it was so closely associated with a woman, Emma Buck. BIA policy operated to exclude women from the public realm and to attempt to restructure Utes' private lives according to Euro-American notions. But Ute women had never been subsidiary to men and the BIA's efforts only created strains and tensions, and agency personnel seem to have been simply oblivious to women's activities. The Bureau set up a matrons' program for most reservations in the West and the Southern Utes were no exception. Its goals were to improve household sanitation, decrease infant mortality, and inculcate Euro-American standards of keeping house, decorating, cleaning, sewing, and cooking. Since most Utes still lived in tepees or tents, the effort was somewhat misplaced. Perhaps the matrons' most important contribution to Southern Ute culture was establishing exhibits and prizes for women's crafts and products such as beadwork, moccasins, quilts, breads, pies, cakes, and quilts, and for the "cleanest baby" that matched the awards for men's products such as garden vegetables, grains, livestock, and poultry, and for the winners of ball games, horse races, and arrow shooting contests.[13]

The year 1920 was the nadir of the Southern Ute population: Economically, Utes had suffered loss of 95% of their land; a generation of assault on their culture and social fabric; and nearly complete dependency on the U.S. Government not only for rations, but even for access to money-funds from the successful 1909 claims lawsuit—that was rightfully theirs. Several smallpox influenza epidemics between 1890 and 1920 had dropped the population to little more than 300. Yet throughout the 1920s Ute language continued to be the lingua franca; Utes continued to look to their own leaders, rather than missionaries, teachers, and Indian agents, for guidance; customs such as use of cradleboards and celebration of the annual Bear Dance in the spring persisted; and Utes replaced and supplemented their indigenous customs not with the religion and worldview of the surrounding Anglos, but rather, with Indian institutions such as the Sun Dance and Peyotism. Up until about 1925, the Warrior Society[14] and its Women's Auxiliary continued to initiate new members and to conduct rituals. The popular Great Basin round dances also continued to be held.

It was during this period of duress that Southern Utes coalesced into a Tribe and despite adopting some Euro-American customs such as living in houses, using privies, and reading and writing English, they remained a distinct socio-cultural island in a sea of non-Indian farmers, ranchers, and miners living and working along the Animas River and its drainages. Southern Utes in the 1930s continued to constitute a distinct, closed corporate community with 100% of the population proficient in the Ute language. They had also assimilated individuals from surrounding Navajo, Jicarilla Apache, and Hispanic populations through marriage and miscegenation. Altogether, Southern Utes probably adopted more Hispanic customs, including learning the Spanish language, nominally becoming Catholics, adopting Hispanic tastes in food and cooking practices, and building structures of adobe or jacal, than they did Anglo ones, despite agents' pressure. It may have been Hispanics, rather than Anglo Indian agents, who contributed the most to Utes' eventually embracing of agriculture, which seems to have been well established by the mid-1930s.[15] Perhaps the most important Anglo cultural custom adopted during this period, however, was the agricultural fair; by the 1960s the annual Ute Fair on the Tribal grounds in Ignacio had become institutionalized as a thoroughly Ute event.

Reorganization

The Indian Reorganization Act (IRA) of 1934 was John Collier's brainchild. Newly appointed as Commissioner of Indian Affairs, a job for which he had lobbied, Collier tried to wrap every single reform that he advocated into one single package—the IRA. The IRA would implement an "Indian New Deal" to parallel Franklin Roosevelt's "New Deal" for the American public as a whole.

As the source of all fundamental historical developments in Indian affairs in the recent past,[16] the "Indian New Deal" altered the means, but not fundamentally the end, of U.S. Indian policy: acculturation and some degree of assimilation.[17] Its context had been established by a devastatingly frank report by the Brookings Institution, commissioned in 1927 by the Secretary of the Interior to investigate and report the administration of Indians. The Report targeted the failure of administrative decrees and policies to successfully guide the quasi-colonized wards of the Government into the American melting pot. It made one thing very clear: the assimilation policy had not only failed to work, but had also plunged Indians into the depths of poverty, illness, short life expectancy, and psychological malaise *because of* the very commitment to enforcing conformity.[18] The Indian New Deal was planned ostensibly to alleviate that situation. Its primary political and administrative implement was the Indian Reorganization Act.

Congress passed the Indian Reorganization Act in 1934. The IRA protected indigenous law, culture, religion, language, education, and artistic and symbolic expression by uniformly lifting any and all bans and barriers on these aspects of

Indian life. Administratively, the BIA began to encourage perpetuation and revival of Indian arts, crafts, cultures, and religions. Thus, "reorganization" envisioned maintenance of much of Indians' traditions, but also clearly envisioned their adoption of a complex of new traits and behavior patterns in economy and politics. The Act's provisions that were directly relevant to the Southern Utes were mainly political and economic. Those provisions called for purchasing new land for existing reservations; setting up an Indian Revolving Loan Fund of $4 million for economic development and credit unions; establishing tribal governments operating by constitutions and by-laws adopted by tribal referendum; and empowering a tribe to hire a lawyer, negotiate with state and federal government, and prevent the sale, lease, disposition, or encumbrance of tribal lands. The Act intended to "reorganize" Indians on two levels: economically, according to a cooperative and corporate model; and politically, as a government for which the Secretary of the Interior would provide checks and balances. Collier's inspiration was the method of "indirect rule" pioneered by Lord Lugard in India and used by British colonial officials in Africa, particularly Nigeria.[19]

The Indian Reorganization Act has been called a "therapeutic exercise" in "responsible democracy" which is dynamogenic, productive of efficiency, and conducive to discipline.[20] But democracy works on the possibility— "almost the habit"—of people forming pressure groups and "cause organizations" and on the assumption that those in power will be accountable to those they claim to represent. Thus, IRA tribes were ultimately pressure groups, hammering out policy by discussion, representation, and consensus, on the basis of choices and alternatives that people had. For Utes, it would mean unlearning nearly every habit of dependency that had been drummed into them during the previous 40 years and using yet another idea that had not been theirs, this time to create and seize opportunities that would secure the future.

Collier did not anticipate bringing the actual law to Indians for their approval; he somehow thought it automatically represented Indians' interests. It was Congress that finally decided to insert a provision that, in order for the IRA to apply to a specific group, the group must approve the Act by majority vote of adults in a referendum. The Act would take effect only if a majority of tribes approved it. Collier held several congresses in or near Indian country in 1933 to explain the Act; in its original form, called the "Wheeler-Howard Bill" after its congressional sponsors, it ran to over 100 pages. Collier sent a 94-page memorandum explaining the bill to every agency superintendent and to a number of anthropologists, including Franz Boas, and to some Indians. He got a number of varying comments on it. But there were far many more who simply had not had enough time to read and understand it by the time the "Indian congresses" were held. Buckskin Charley and other Southern Ute leaders expressed opposition to it initially, but when it came to a vote in 1935, Charley supported it and the IRA passed by a vote of 85 to 10 out of a voting population of 129. Thus, the vote represented a 73% participation rate and a 66% approval rate.[21]

Southern Utes approved a Constitution in 1936 and adopted a Corporate Charter in 1938. Buckskin Charley died in 1935, but when the first Council convened in 1937, it elected his son, Antonio Buck, as the first Chairman of the Southern Ute Council. Thus the process of IRA acceptance at Southern Ute seems to have been both a reflection of and a validation for the coalescence of tribal unity that occurred under the Buck Chieftaincy.

Although most Americans remember the Great Depression as a decade of unprecedented hardship, for Utes, it was the *end* of nearly four decades of unprecedented hardship. In 1938 the BIA succeeded in getting 200,000 acres of "public domain"—largely timbered mesa-top land that Anglos had not homesteaded—returned to the Southern.[22] Since that time, an additional 64,100 acres have been either returned or have been purchased by the Tribe, and the reservation now encompasses 307,000 acres.

In 1933 the Civilian Conservation Corps-Indian Division initiated the first of over 100 projects on the Southern Ute Reservation that resulted in the expenditure of $558,000 between 1933 and 1942. In 1960, 48 persons in a survey of the 220 adults living on the Reservation were found to have participated in the work carried out by the CCC.[23] A cooperative sheep herd and a Credit Association were established, and although the sheep herd failed in the late 1940s, as did a short-lived Tribal Cattle Enterprise and Farm during the 1950s, the efforts represented the first tangible attempts by the BIA to help the Utes help themselves without peddling its own agenda.

The IRA's most significant legacy came as a result of the return of the 200,000 acres that had not been lost to homesteading and the capacity for the Southern Ute Tribe to hire its own attorney. Much of the returned acreage turned out to contain gas and oil reserves. Under another piece of "New Deal" legislation, the Indian Mineral Leasing Act of 1938, the Tribe let its first mineral leases in 1950. In 1938 the Southern Ute Tribe joined the adjacent Mountain Utes and the Ute Tribe of Utah in a lawsuit filed in the U.S. Court of Claims for damages and monetary compensation for land taken in the previous century. In 1951, $5,752,035 from a favorable judgment in this Claims case was dispersed to the Southern Utes[24] and the Tribal government used the money not only for per capita payments to its citizens, but also for an ambitious program of home improvements, agricultural assistance, emergency family assistance, and trust funds for children.[25]

But just as things started to get better, things started to get worse. Budget constraints brought by World War II discouraged Collier and led him to resign in 1945. Congress set up a Commission chaired by former president Herbert Hoover to investigate Indian affairs. In 1948 the Hoover Commission issued its report, proposing steps "to integrate the Indians into the rest of the population as the best solution to 'the Indian problem.'" In a complete reversal of policy, the second in less than two decades, federal attitudes towards Indians again changed course. Assimilation was to be the dominant goal of public policy. The new policy represented a return to the past, an abandonment of bilateralism; thus it proceeded without Indian cooperation. "In an effort to relieve itself once and for all of the financial and moral burden of Indian affairs, the federal government reasserted full control of Indian lives and fortunes and fit them into its plan. It was a lousy plan," says sociologist Stephen Cornell.[26]

The thrust of this "lousy plan" was now directed toward preparing all Indians for termination of federal trust responsibility; abolishing reservations; and providing assistance for nuclear families, rather than communities, to become integrated into the dominant society either by being trained for wage jobs near reservations or by being relocated to cities. The plan was called "termination" because federal services to Indians, federal trusteeship over Indians and their resources, reservations, and Tribes eventually would be "terminated." Senators Patrick McCarran (Nevada) and Arthur B. Watkins (Utah) were among those who pushed hardest for termination legislation. Watkins phrased the aim in terms of "freeing" the Indians "from the yoke of federal supervision."[27] Several developments contributed both to the acceleration of this thrust and to Indians' successful opposition to it.[28]

Assistance to Indians wishing to relocate to cities had been an option under the Indian New Deal. Under the termination policy, relocation became virtually a mandate. Relocation to cities was an especially disheartening experience for many Southern Utes, although not for all. The relocation program was especially aimed at returning veterans. Provided with an apartment, job training, and employment in one of several cities—Denver, Salt Lake City, Chicago, Oakland, Los Angeles—the Indian client was expected to become an average, urban-dwelling wage-earner within six months. But by the late 1950s, many relocatees had returned home after experiencing layoffs, discrimination, inadequate preparation for city life, and alienation from kin and culture.

These younger heads of families—in their 30s, 40s, and 50s—sought alternatives within stagnating reservation milieus and unpromising economies. Termination, however, was not one of those alternatives. The Civilian Conservation Corps had been important in serving as a kind of proving ground for persons who later became leaders in the Southern Ute Tribal Council and some of these young leaders had also been lured into the urban relocation program, only to return home after being disillusioned. They had knowledge and experience of three important phases of Southern Ute life: the dismal, hardscrabble life of their childhoods; the challenging and optimistic era of the Indian New Deal; and the disheartening and disappointing process of termination that stripped many Native Americans of their dignity and heritage while failing to provide them with viable income or social identity within the urban milieu.

These leaders took decisive action during the termination era. Every tribe was to be placed in one of two categories: to be terminated, or to be "rehabilitated" for termination. Many tribes such as the Southern Paiutes of Utah and a good number in Oregon and California were simply put into the termination category without being consulted. But tribes with large reservations and prominence in the history of BIA actions were given a choice. The Southern Utes were given the choice. They categorically rejected termination. Thus they were slated for "rehabilitation."

Rehabilitation was cast in primarily economic terms. Southern Utes were required to use substantial amounts of their own money from claims awards and oil and gas leases for rehabilitation. But Tribes could still obtain funds through the BIA for road and range improvement and for timber, fish, and game management. Therefore, in 1953, the Tribe drew up an impressive "long range plan." The plan included proposals for establishing administrative departments that would parallel the BIA's administration, including a forestry department, a range department, a roads departments, an agricultural committee, and a branch of land operations.[29] The Tribe also took over maintenance of the tribal roll, which had been kept by the Bureau since 1880 when treaty annuities were first dispersed and later as a check on eligibility for rations through a "Tribal membership" committee. When the BIA stopped providing medical services in 1955 and closed the local hospital, the Southern Utes quickly negotiated an agreement with Blue Cross-Blue Shield for provision of medical insurance and made a bid to take over the old hospital building. They had it renovated and moved the Tribal offices into it.

Subsequent long range plans were developed in 1956, 1958, 1960, 1964, 1966, 1968, and 1974. Nearly all the goals of these plans were reached. They included establishing social services, welfare, and education committees (later Tribal departments); a college scholarship program; a summer day camp for children; and an alcoholic treatment program. In 1957, when the Public Health Service began moving into many Indian reservations to provide medical services that had been closed by the BIA, the Southern Ute Tribe made recommendations for specific treatment programs and clinics that eventually resulted in a "Southern Ute" public health clinic being established with region-wide responsibilities. The Tribe established a "Custom Farm" program which provided equipment and labor at minimal cost to Tribal members, and another program to put 8,000 acres of irrigable land under irrigation. Forest management was improved; range conservation and management were implemented on a systematic basis; reservoirs were constructed and stocking ponds excavated; and fencing, reseeding, and erosion control programs were begun. When the Bureau proposed terminating the Ute Vocational Boarding School in 1956, the Tribe became a partner in a consolidated public school district that included the Ignacio Boarding School, which the Tribe took over under a consolidation contract from the BIA utilizing Johnson-O'Malley funds.

In 1958 the Tribe completely revamped its judicial procedures and the Tribal law and order code. It had moved quickly to establish a Tribal Court in 1938 that took over from the Court of Indian Offenses. But taking the initiative in the law and order field provided the Tribal Council not only with complete independence to appoint judges, but also control over the police force. The Tribe also developed a procedure for Tribal members to apply for home sites, and guaranteed provision of infrastructure such as water, electricity, and graded roads to the home sites. In 1960 the Tribe implemented big game hunting along with a program for managing the two elk herds on the reservation. While hunting permits were free to Tribal members, non-Tribal members would have to pay a fee more or less equivalent to fees on U.S. Forests, most of which have little in the way of elk. The program was so successful that by the 1980s it was not only financing operation of the Tribe's Fish and Game Department, but also making a sizable profit.

Under the Tribe's management, the range, farming, timber, and social programs operated more efficiently and with more vigor than they ever had under the BIA. Despite a steady downturn in the viability of farming in most areas of the United States beginning in 1920, farming was more successful among the Southern Utes in the 1960s than it had ever been.[30] But achieving the overall goal of a diversified, stable reservation economy that would maintain a standard of living comparable to the United States in general still eluded the Tribe no matter what it did. Several coal companies, including Peabody and Sunoco, dangled lucrative possibilities in front of the Tribe, proposing to start open pit mining of coal reserves in the Fruitland formation that crops out on the eastern and southwestern portions of the reservation. But despite numerous feasibility studies conducted by these companies, by the BIA and USGS, and by the Tribe itself throughout the 1960s, 1970s, and 1980s, coal development remained an unconvincing alternative.

The Great Society

Tourism was another matter. In 1964, President Lyndon Johnson accelerated the "Great Society" programs such as Head Start and inaugurated others. The Comprehensive Education and Training Act (CETA) provided not only training, but also part-time employment. The Indian Youth Corps and Job Corps also provided employment. A Southern Ute Housing Authority was established and began building houses, first on Tribal assignments, and later in clusters, at low cost. The Housing Authority also built an apartment complex in the city of Ignacio itself. The Southern Ute Community Action Program (SUCAP) was also established in the "Great Society" era and began providing services, training, employment, and emergency medical services. The net impact of these programs on Indian reservations was not only to make them more attractive places to live and thus stop the out-migration hemorrhaging, but also to effectively reverse termination. Never officially repudiated, the policy was nonetheless quietly abandoned as first Johnson, and then Nixon and Ford, placed an emphasis on funding local community development and partially decentralizing federal control of funds and programs.

The Utes now found themselves in an ironic situation. Having tenaciously hung on to homeland, tribal organization, and cultural identity, they now had to share the "Great Society" programs of which they were the focus with the surrounding Hispanic and Anglo populations, which now outnumbered Utes by more than three to one. Head Start, Community Action, School, and Housing Authority boards had to have representation from the entire community, and Utes found themselves often outnumbered on these decision-making bodies. They had regained control over their own Tribal affairs, but they had only partially regained control over their reservation and the communities on it.

Most importantly, Utes found themselves with little control over the reservation economy. All retail outlets of every sort were operated by non-Indians. Tribal enterprises seemed to operate only within the Tribal organization, with the exception of the Big Game hunting program. Tribal resources such as range lands, timber, oil, and gas were under lease to non-Indians largely on their conditions, not the Tribe's. Did tourism hold any economic potential? The scenic beauty of the reservation and recent areas had recently gotten a boost through the filming of *Around the World in Eighty Days* and nearly the entire Tribe had turned out as extras for the "Indian scenes" in the movie. The popularity of Mesa Verde National Park was on the increase, and there was some potential for attracting visitors to unusual geologic formations such as Chimney Rock and to Navajo Reservoir, which provided water for the San Juan-Chama project at the expense of two small communities of Hispanics and Utes that had been flooded by it: Rosa and Tiffany. Was it possible that the Tribe might develop a tourist facility which it alone would run and manage for profit, that would bring money into the area and that would not compete with some already existing enterprise, and that would provide employment exclusively for Tribal members?

Tourist facilities were high on the priority list of the Johnson Administration. Beginning in 1963, the Commerce Department's Area Redevelopment Administration conducted a number of feasibility studies of tourist potential on many Indian reservations. One of them was the Southern Ute Reservation. Additionally, the Office of Economic Opportunity provided grants for feasibility studies to any federally funded agency that submitted a reasonable proposal. Between 1963 and 1970, it provided funding for the study of more than half a dozen ideas for the Southern Ute Reservation. In addition, the Tribal Council came up with several ideas of its own.

Between 1963 and 1966 the following projects were proposed: para-mutual horse racing; purchase of a lake for recreation purposes; development of a dude ranch; a restaurant-motel complex; a ski area; an "exclusive use" shooting preserve; a summerlong "Indian city" theme park; and development of a Chimney Rock tourist facility. The Tribal Council had the wisdom to explore but not adopt most of these proposals. Only the lake and the restaurant-motel complex projects were implemented. Part of Lake Capote was eventually set aside for tourist camping, but it was used primarily for Tribal recreation and summer youth camps. The Pino-Nuche motel and restaurant was eventually completed close to Tribal headquarters but despite proximity to Durango, ski runs, and a scenic railroad, it attracted few tourists. For more than a decade it operated at a loss, in some years sustaining huge losses. But by the early 1980s careful management and a growing clientele among Utes and non-Utes for the bar and restaurant had resulted in it making a modest profit. The Big Game hunting program was coordinated with Pino-Nuche operations so that hunters could get a package deal with their hunting permit that included lodging in the motel and meals, including sack lunches while hunting. Advertisement of the complex for conventions among BIA, law enforcement, and other agencies also began bringing more clients.

Southern Ute dollars continued to flow out of the reservation, however, to nearby towns: Durango, Farmington, and even to Ignacio. In yet another attempt to keep dollars circulating longer among Southern Utes, the Tribe constructed a general store in 1984. Huge losses forced its closure a few years later. The store sold groceries as well as dry goods and hardware. Although not profitable (nor intended to be), it represented yet another effort by Southern Utes to recapture the economic independence that they once had and quickly lost during the disastrous allotment period. It would take a combination of federal cooperation and a state-wide referendum to provide a venue for Ute entrepreneurship to move toward economic stability through tourism.

Self-Determination

In 1975 Congress officially implemented the self-determination policy for Indian Tribes. Rather than having to wrestle the local BIA agency for control over programs and contracts, Tribes would be encouraged to take over BIA services and programs under contract. Having already taken their future in hand when nobody thought they had one, Southern Utes were unusually well prepared to take over just about every BIA program, and did so.

Several amendments to the Tribal Constitution made important changes in the Tribe's political process, also in 1975. Adopted by referendum vote, they reflected the most major alterations since adoption of the Constitution in 1937. One changed the nature of the offices of Chairman and Vice-Chairman. Rather than being elected from the body of the Tribal Council, the Chairman and Vice-Chairman were to be elected at large on one ticket for a two-year term. Any single candidate would be limited to four terms in succession. Another amendment provided for any measure not passed by the Tribal Council unanimously to be put to a vote of the eligible voters in referendum upon recommendation of a member of the Council or submission of a petition from voters with the requisite number of signatures. Yet a third change took the Tribe's blood-quantum requirement from one-half down to one-quarter. This change resulted in the enrollment of many individuals who categorize themselves as "Spanish Southern Ute." They are the products of marriages between the sons and daughters of Hispanics who married Southern Utes that had one Hispanic parent. The intermarriage of Utes and Hispanics has been going on for more than a century and a half, accelerating after about 1880, and many products of Ute-Hispanic marriages were as comfortable in Ute society as in Hispanic, and often equally knowledgeable of the culture, customs, and language of both groups. Thus the possibility of Tribal enrollment for Spanish Southern Utes amounted to a legal recognition of a long-standing socio-cultural fact.

Economic Stability

Economic stability remained elusive throughout the 1970s and 1980s. Although establishment of a Tribal oil and gas department brought hundreds of thousands of additional dollars into Tribal coffers as a result of replacing BIA and USGS oversight with more careful Tribal monitoring and accounting procedures, mean household incomes were less than half those of surrounding non-Indians in 1980, and the percentage of families below poverty level was a whopping 37% in contrast to 7.3% for surrounding non-Indian households and 11.2% for the U.S. as a whole. Labor force participation was one-third less for Southern Utes than for the surrounding population, and unemployment was running at 57%.[31] By 1989 things had improved, but were still problematic. Per capita income was $6,124 as opposed to $12,163 for surrounding La Plata County. The percent of persons with incomes below poverty level had dropped from 39.9% in 1980 to 31% in 1989, but unemployment levels in 1989 seemed to be nearly identical to those of 1989.[31,32] Of those who were employed, 80% worked for either the Tribal Government, federal agencies, or Tribally owned enterprises.

The 1990s brought the most far-reaching economic changes since the Indian New Deal. After two decades of negotiations among the federal and state governments, the Ute Mountain and Southern Ute Tribes agreed to a compromise agreement concerning their water rights in 1986. Eleven major streams and rivers flow out of the San Juan-La Plata ranges and the Sangre de Cristo Mountains onto the two reservations. Legally, the two Tribes have rights to as much water from those streams as they need. The Tribes agreed, however, to relinquish rights to water in all the streams that they were not already using in exchange for control over specified amounts of water from the Delores, Las Animas and La Plata rivers. In 1988 Congress authorized completion of the Delores Water Project, begun in the 1970s, that would bring water to the Ute

Mountain Tribe, and also provided money for economic development, essentially as a buy-out of the Tribes' water rights.

In 2000, Congress funded a scaled-down Animas-La Plata Project to secure water in reservoirs for the Southern Ute Tribe as well as other potential users. First conceptualized and proposed in the 1940s, the Project was put on hold for many years, even after Congress authorized it in 1968, pending settlement of Tribal water claims. Supporters saw it as a way for the Southern Utes to secure the actual water flowing through the reservation that they legally claimed but could not use without reservoirs and irrigation facilities. Opponents saw it as an Army Corps of Engineers dinosaur, left over from the era of willy-nilly dam-building that flooded wildernesses and destroyed ecosystems. Although a long-standing goal of Sam Maynes, the Southern Ute Tribe's attorney, support for the Project among Tribal members began to erode in the 1990s just as victory for its implementation was imminent. Opponents, Indian and non-Indian, argued that the Project was unnecessary; that its costs had arisen to astronomical levels that could not be justified; that the radical ecological changes entailed in damming the river defied the principles of environmental stewardship that should guide Indians' approach to managing natural resources; and that the purposes envisioned for the Project were obsolete. Increasingly fewer Utes made their livings from farming, argued the opponents, and the need for irrigation water that had initially been the Project's impetus was no longer supportable.

Several studies done in the environmental assessment phase of the Project supported some of these claims: it was found that it could pose a threat to two species of fish and the costs of construction hardly justified the minimal benefit in terms of agricultural production. Moreover, insisted the opponents, the much-touted agricultural uses that were projected served merely as a smokescreen for what were covert municipal and industrial interests: the water would be purchased to turn more of La Plata County into retirement and vacation home sites and golf courses and would also finally make exploitation of coal resources on the Southern Ute Reservation economically feasible. The water could be used to supply cooling towers for a coal-fired power plant, they pointed out, and with energy demand on the rise, the real reason for promoting the Animas-La Plata Project had nothing to do with implementing Indian water rights; in reality it had become part of a scheme by industrial interests to move forward with the last phase of a plan to place fossil-fueled electricity production facilities on the Colorado Plateau to transmit power to Las Vegas, Los Angeles, and other megalopolises of the west without urban air quality restrictions.

The Animas-La Plata Project emerged as an issue in elections for Tribal Council seats and for the position of Tribal Chairman. Despite the election of vocal opponents of the Project, however, the official position of the Southern Ute Tribe did not change: the Tribe continued to support the Project and Colorado's Senator Ben Nighthorse Campbell, a Northern Cheyenne who had lived and worked as an artist in Ignacio, continued to press for going ahead with the Project. Because much of the work on the Project would be contracted to the Southern Ute and Ute Mountain Tribes, the Project's initial impact locally was projected to be positive: unemployment would ease; family incomes would rise; and young people would stay at home. Although opposition continues from within the Tribe and without, initial work on the Project has begun.

The Future

Two other economic developments may ultimately prove more lucrative than either agriculture or coal mining and electricity production. These are oil and gas production and gambling. The Tribe had brought a high-powered manager into the Tribal administration from the oil and gas industry in the 1980s to improve the Tribe's oversight of oil and gas royalties managed by the Bureau of Indian Affairs and U.S. Geological Survey. The expertise resulting from training Tribal members through this strategy enabled establishment of a Tribally owned production company. In a precedent-setting move, Red Willow Production Company negotiated an agreement in 1993 to actually operate a number of the gas wells on the Reservation, thereby making the Tribe a partner in production rather than just a collector of royalties. This arrangement also brought Tribal members into the energy industry workforce, where employment of Utes had previously been negligible or non-existent.

The Sky Ute Casino may prove to have the greatest economic impact of any recent endeavor. Opening in 1993, the Casino was an instant huge success. Authorized by the Indian Gaming Act of 1988, blackjack, slot-machine, roulette, and other high stakes gambling became legal on Indian reservations as long as such gambling was not prohibited by state laws. Colorado authorized highstakes gambling by a referendum passed in 1990. Presently Towaoc and Ignacio Mountain are two of only five places in the state where high stakes gambling is available and not surprisingly, the Sky Ute Casino returned a quicker profit on investment than even the purchase of partial ownership in the gas wells. And while energy production is a low-labor industry, gambling is not. The Sky Ute Lodge and Casino is the largest single employer of Tribal members other than the Tribal administration itself.

Culture and People

Despite their unusually successful collective management of their journey back from the dismal situation of the 1920s, Southern Utes still face significant challenges in the twenty first century. Pan-Indianism has brought pow-wows and there has been some revival of nineteenth-century dance rituals. Elders still command respect in the Tribe, and through the "Elders' Council," they have been able to maintain considerable influence in the Tribe's social and political affairs. Implementation of the Native American Graves Protection and

Repatriation Act (1990) has granted renewed influence to individuals who can speak with authority about cultural traditions as museums throughout the country search their collections to identify human remains and funerary items dug up from burials that are potentially returnable to Utes and other Tribes under the law. The round dance is still seen on occasion but while the Sun Dance shows every sign of maintaining itself as a vigorous religious institution and the Bear Dance remains a popular pan-Ute celebration, other aspects of traditional culture are in danger of being lost.

But there are no longer any shamans among either of the Colorado Ute Tribes, paralleling situations among other Great Basin Tribes such as the Western Shoshone, among whom there is only one practicing shaman. And the singers for Bear Dances and Sun Dances are mostly in their 50s and 60s, with Sun Dance chiefs being middle-aged or older. Although Ute is still commonly spoken among the Mountain Utes, no Southern Ute under the age of 40 speaks Ute fluently, and until the 1990s an increasing number of younger people did not understand the language at all. Although interest in beading has taken an upsurge in recent years, other traditional technological expertise such as the processing of willow for basketry; making of baskets; tanning of hides; and making of buckskin garments and footwear, once widespread, is now limited to a few specialists, as is knowledge of traditional medicine and plant use. However, the Tribe's establishment of a "Ute Academy" for the specific purpose of teaching Tribal customs and language might reverse the erosion of cultural knowledge as young people are presented with an opportunity for learning the language and cultural traditions of their ancestors in the setting of a standard educational setting.

Because half the Southern Ute population is under the age of 18 as compared to one-fourth of the population of the U.S. in general and Ute families are about 40% larger than the typical U.S. household, the size and composition of Ute families "has important implications for future employment demands, the demand for social services, and the economic strain placed on families who have few resources but contain a great number of dependent families."[33] Four times as many families (40.2%) are likely to be headed by women among the Southern Ute population as among the U.S. population generally and despite a tradition tending toward matrifocality, the fact that among Ute Mountain Utes the rate is 90% *less* and among Northern Utes still only a little more than half as common,[32] the statistic indicates that the same factors promoting matrifocality among Southern Utes may be the same ones that promote matrifocality among other North American minority populations with large proportions under poverty-level: high dependence on welfare payments to dependent children; the necessity for men to be employed away from home; and a degree of poverty that results in female kindred sharing child-caring responsibilities.[34]

The demographic situation alone indicates that Southern Utes may be facing future challenges just as great as those of the early part of the twentieth century.

Fewer than two-thirds of the 1,200 Southern Utes live on the reservation, with nearly 300 living on other Indian reservations or in cities such as Denver, Farmington, Albuquerque, or Salt Lake City. The long-sought Animas-LaPlata and Delores water projects may or may not bring the long-anticipated benefits of large-scale Tribal agriculture, but if the Casino avoids the managerial volatility that seems inherent in the gambling industry, it may prove to be the biggest factor in halting the diaspora.

The Tribe's successful implementation of a severance tax ordinance as well as its careful management of capital producing sufficient dividends to partially finance the tribal administration; provide funds for further investment; and yield per capita payments to individuals amounting to several hundred dollars in most years are outcomes that attest to the wisdom of Tribal leaders. But managing increased Tribal revenue and larger per capita payments brings its own challenges, as does managing highly capitalized industries such as oil and gas production and casino operation. The damage done by the federal allotment and assimilation policies of the early part of the twentieth century and the often insensitive, incompetent, unscrupulous, and unremittingly rigid local BIA administrators during that same time period made it doubly hard for Utes to steer a course through the turbulent 1950s and 1960s when claims settlements and oil and gas development suddenly gave people money who had had no money before. Continuing to steer a judicious course through an increasingly unpredictable and volatile global political economic channel will probably make Southern Ute Tribalness and Tribal cohesion an even more crucially important asset for the viability of Southern Ute individuals than ever before.

Notes

For details on documents labeled ARCIA and FRC, see Abbreviations.

Chapter 1: The Crucible

1.   Carl Schurz, *Report of the Secretary of the Interior* (Washington, D.C: Government Printing Office, 1877), 9-12.

2.   Omer C. Stewart, *Ethnohistorical Bibliography of the Ute Indians of Colorado* (Boulder: University of Colorado Press, 1971).

3.   Frances L. Swadesh, *Los Primeros Pobladores: Hispanic Americans of the Ute Frontier* (Notre Dame: University of Notre Dame Press, 1974).

4.   Frances L. Quintana, *Pobladores: Hispanic Americans of the Ute Frontier* (Aztec: Frances Leon Quintana, 1991).

5.   Edward Spicer, "Yaqui Religious Acculturation," *American Anthropologist,* 60 (1958.): 433-441.

6.   Melville Herskovits, *Acculturation* (Gloucester: Peter Smith, 1938).

7.   Omer C. Stewart, *Ute Indians: Before and After White Contact,* Institute of Behavioral Science at Boulder. Boulder: University of Colorado Press 56 (1966): 43.

Chapter 2: The Context of Change

1.   FRC 44014-005/130—4/27/1877 (*Records of Southern Ute Agency, 1877-1952.* National Archives No. RG 75. Federal Records Center, Denver, Colorado).

2.   FRC 44014-005/123—3/25/1878.

3.   FRC 44014-005/130—6/11/1877.

4.   FRC 44014-005/130—12/15/1877.

5.   FRC 44014-005/130—1/22/1878.

6.   FRC 44014-005/130—1/1/1878)

7.   ARCIA 1877: 2 (*Annual Report of the Commissioner of Indian Affairs* to the Secretary of the Interior).

8.   FRC 44014-005/130—2/7/1878.

9.   FRC 44014-005/130—6/26/1878.

10.   FRC 44014-005/130—8/27/1878.

11.   FRC 44014-005/130—2/14/1878.

12.   FRC 44014-005/130—9/19/1878.

13.   FRC 44014-005/130—10/2/1878.

14.   FRC 44014-005/060—10/18/1879.

15.   FRC 44014-005/125—10/15/1879.

16.   FRC 44094-005/301—4/22/1878.

17.   FRC 44014-005/060—12/12/1879.

18.   FRC 44014-005/060—1/12/1880.

19.   ARCIA 1880: 24.

20.   ARCIA 1880: 194.

21.   ARCIA 1880: 23-24.

22.   FRC 44014-005/121—7/14/1882.

23. FRC 44014-005/121—6/13/1882.
24. FRC 44014-005/175—2/28/1883.
25. FRC 44014-005/121—1/30/1882.
26. FRC 44014-005/120—12/24/1879.
27. FRC 44014-005/125—7/20/1884.
28. ARCIA 1885: 14.
29. FRC 44014-005/125—11/26/1885.
30. FRC 44014-005/060—8/9/1885.
31. ARCIA 1887: 16.
32. FRC 44014-005/060— 1/16/1886.
33. U.S. Congress. Senate. *Senate Report, Number 836,* 49th Congress, 1st Session, Washington, D.C: Government Printing Office, 1886.
34. FRC 44014-005/304—8/24/1888.
35. Report of Southern Ute Commission (U.S. Congress. Senate. *Report of Southern Ute Commission, 1889*: Report of Chairman, Secretary's Journal and Commissioner J. J. Enright's Report on Agreement with Southern Utes, Sen. Exec. Doc., 50th Congress, 2d Session, Washington, D.C: Government Printing Office, 1889).
36. FRC 44014-005/094—4/14/1890.
37. FRC 44105-005/806—3/2/1892.
38. FRC 44105-005/806g—8/19/1892.
39. FRC 44105-005/806g—11/14/1892.
40. FRC 44015-Lyon—11/21/1892.
41. FRC 44015-006 Lyon—11/29/1892.
42. ARCIA 1893.
43. U.S. Bureau of the Census, *11th Census, Report on Indians Taxed and Not Taxed* (Washington, D.C: Government Printing Office, 1890) (George Meston Report).
44. U.S. Congress. House. H. R. Committee Reports, *House Committee Report, Number 1205*, 52d Congress, 1st Session, Washington, D.C: Government Printing Office, 1892.
45. ARCIA Board of Indian Commissioners 1896: 20.
46. U.S. Congress. House. *Report of House Committee on Indian Affair (Mr. Hunter),* to accompany H.R.6742, 53d Congress, 2d Session, Washington, D.C: Government Printing Office, 1894.
47. ARCIA 1895: 138-141
48. Tri-Ethnic Microfilm Roll #6-FRC Roll #V-Frame 739—4/20/1895.
49. ARCIA Board of Indian Commissioners 1896.

Chapter 3: Consequences of Allotment

1. FRC 44014-005/130—2/14/1878.
2. FRC 44094-005/308—11/9/1877, 2/3/1878 and 4/22/1878.
3. FRC 44014-005/130—5/11/1878.
4. FRC 44094-005/301—11/19/1877.
5. FRC 44094-005/301—12/27/1877.
6. FRC 44014-005/130—4/5/1878.
7. FRC 44094-005/320—3/27/1896.

8. ARCIA 1895: 140.
9. FRC 44094-005/340—11/27/1886.
10. FRC 44094-005/340—6/20/1887.
11. FRC 44094-005/377—10/31/1895 and 5/7/1896.
12. FRC 44094-005/377—12/16/1895.
13. FRC 44094-005/340—8/19/1902.
14. ARCIA 1896: 133.
15. FRC 44094-005/340—4/14/1908.
16. FRC 44094-005/310—Letterbook, p. 67—4/10/1910.
17. FRC 44014-005/092—10/16/1902.
18. FRC 44094-005/310-Letterbook-1910.
19. FRC 44016-050—1911, p. 25.
20. FRC 44105-005/910b—4/1/1912.
21. FRC 44019-161 Day—8/18/1913.
22. FRC 44017-154/060—3/24/1926.
23. FRC 44017-154/160—3/25/1926.
24. FRC 44018-005 Beaumont and FRC 44019-005 Page.
25. ARCIA 1880: p. 17.
26. FRC 44014-005/130—5/30/1878 and 7/5/1878.
27. FRC 44094-005/304—8/24/1888.
28. George Meston Report 1890: 225.
29. ARCIA 1895: p. 141.
30. FRC 44094-005/377—1909.
31. FRC 44094-005/377—10/29/1901.
32. FRC 44094-005/340—2/10/1926.
33. FRC 44094-005/340—9/5/1907.
34. FRC 44011-Letterbook b, insert between pp. 131 and 132—12/29/1903.
35. FRC 44014-005/150—5/6/1905.
36. FRC 44094-005/340—undated, 1908?
37. FRC 44094-005/340—2/10/1926, 2/15/1926, 3/20/1926, and 5/15/1926.
38. FRC 44094-005/340—5/19/1926.
39. FRC 44019-005— Leonard, Werner.
40. FRC 44105-005/910b—6/13/1913.
41. FRC 44019-005-Werner—7/23/1909.
42. FRC 44094-005/377—2/17/1912.
43. FRC 44094-005/340—7/26/1913.
44. FRC 44015-005/006—9/27/1911.
45. FRC 44015-006 Richards—9/30/1912.
46. FRC 44014-005/124—2/25/1918 and 6/27/1918.
47. FRC 44014-005/124—7/27/1910.
48. FRC 44015-006—Watts—9/22/1917.
49. FRC 44015-006 Peña—9/4/1917.
50. George Meston Report 1890: 229.
51. Tri-Ethnic Microfilm Roll #6-FRC roll #V, unsigned report, Finance—12/7/1892.
52. FRC 44016-050—1913, p. 2.

53. FRC 44014-005/124—5/21/1913.
54. FRC 44019-161-Moffitt—6/13/1913, 6/20/1913, and 8/4/1913.
55. FRC 44084-250-Annuity Subvouchers—1882-1889.
56. FRC 44094-005/380/—8/30/1899.
57. FRC 44094-005/350—3/9/1914 and 3/31/1914.
58. FRC 44094-005/350—8/4/1917.
59. FRC 44014-005/124—6/24/1886.
60. FRC 44014-005/124—4/14/1892.
61. FRC 44014-005/150—5/6/1905.
62. FRC 44014-005/124—6/27/1913.
63. FRC 44094-005/380—6/6/1907.
64. See particularly FRC 44022-Authorities 1877-1899, for funds and projects deferred or denied.
65. FRC 44014-005/121—9/25/1889.
66. FRC 44014-005/047.

Chapter 4: Crisis: "Self-Support"

1. FRC 44014-005/130—3/20/1878.
2. FRC 44014-005/130—4/27/1878.
3. FRC 44105-005/910a—12/3/1892.
4. FRC 44105-005/910a—7/11/1878.
5. FRC 44014-005/130—9/20/1878.
6. FRC 44105-005/910a—5/26/1880.
7. FRC 44105-005/910a—6/1/1883 and 6/14/1883.
8. See FRC 44022-202.2a Beef Authorities for 1883-1884.
9. See FRC 44022-202.2c Authorities for feed 1880-1890.
10. FRC 44022-202.1c.
11. FRC 44022-202.1c—2/17/1887.
12. FRC 44015-006.
13. FRC 44014-212/006—4/5/1881.
14. FRC 44084-212/250—9/24/1890.
15. FRC 44018-160—Indian Police, nominations approved, 1886-1890.
16. Southern Ute Commission 1889: 29-39.
17. FRC 44018-160—Employee Changes.
18. FRC 44022-202/226—5/1/1886.
19. FRC 44022-202/226—6/22/1889 and 6/26/1889.
20. ARCIA 1893: 132-134.
21. FRC 44014-005/121—12/16/1886.
22. FRC 44105-005/910a—3/12/1885.
23. FRC 44105-005/910a—3/30/1886.
24. FRC 44022—202.2e—7/23/1884.
25. FRC 44022-202.2e—10/31/1906.
26. FRC 44023-005/210—5/8/1912 and 5/13/1912.
27. 44011-Letterbook d, pp. 146-147—9/24/1906.
28. ARCIA 1900: 6-7.

29. FRC 44011-Letterbook a, pp. 9-10—4/4/1900.
30. FRC 44011-Letterbook a, pp. 414-415—9/30/1900.
31. FRC 44105-005/910a—12/21/1891.
32. FRC 44022-202.1c—3/21/1903.
33. FRC 44105-005/910a—11/30/1908.
34. FRC 44105-005/910b—4/11/1912.
35. FRC 44105-005/910b—1/13/1913.
36. FRC 44019-161-Velásquez—9/24/1912.
37. FRC 44019-161-Velásquez—11/22/1912.
38 FRC 44019-161-Velásquez—3/21/1913.
39. FRC 44019-161-Velásquez—5/21/1913 and 8/30/1913.
40. FRC 44017-064—11/5/1896.
41. FRC 44017-173/064—5/23/1910.
42. FRC 44017-154/064—4/15/1926.
43. FRC 44105-005/910b—4/2/1913, 4/3/1913, and 4/7/1913.
44. FRC 44105-005/910b—4/17/1913.
45. FRC 44105-005/910b—4/13/1913.
46. FRC 44105-005/910b—4/30/1913.
47. FRC 44105-005/910b—5/9/1913 and 5/16/1913.
48. FRC 44105-005/910b—5/20/1913.
49. FRC 44105-005/910b—7/21/1913.
50. FRC 44105-005/910b—7/23/1913 and 8/4/1813.
51. FRC 44105-005/ 910b—8/20/1913.
52. FRC 44105-005/910b—9/19/1913.
53. FRC 44105-005/910b—10/11/1913 and 10/28/1913.
54. FRC 44105-005/910b—11/14/1913.
55. FRC 44105-005/910b—11/18/1913.
56. FRC 44105-005/910b—12/13/1913.
57. FRC 44105-005/910b—12/5/1913.
58. FRC 44105-005/910b—2/14/1914.
59. FRC 44105-005/910b—4/15/1914.
60. FRC 44023-005/210—4/1/1914.
61. FRC 44105-005/910b—4/5/1914.
62. FRC 44105-005/910b—4/5/1914.
63. FRC 44105-005/910b—8/24/1914, 9/4/1914, and 9/12/1914.
64. FRC 44016-050—1921.
65. FRC 44105-005/910b—4/24/1918.
66. FRC 44015-005/060—3/24/1926.
67. FRC 44014-154/064—12/8/1925.
68. FRC 44105-005/980—1907-1911.
69. FRC 44105-005/910b—6/18/1913.
70. FRC 44105-005/980—6/19/1913.
71. FRC 44103-005/600—1/5/1918.

Chapter 5: Statistics of Change

1. FRC 44016—050.

Chapter 6: Elements of Contact Relations

1. FRC 44014-005/130—7/1/1878.
2. FRC 44014-005/125—3/6/1887.
3. George Meston Report 1890: 229.
4. FRC 44014-005/121—9/9/1887.
5. FRC 44015-006 Moav—5/11/1918.
6. ARCIA 1881: 24.
7. FRC 44014-005/096—6/9/1926.
8. FRC 44019-161 Valdez—12/16/1877.
9. FRC 44014-005/130—3/14/1878.
10. FRC 44014-005/126—10/12/1880.
11. FRC 44014-005/126—1881-1926.
12. FRC 44018-161 Jeantet et al.—4/2/1903.
13. FRC 44018-161 Manzanares—6/8/1904.
14. FRC 44022-202/226—3/29/1904.
15. See FRC 44018-160—1878-1921.
16. FRC 44019-161 Ulibarri—7/30/1925.
17. See FRC 44013-052/700—6/1890.
18. FRC 44105-005/803—11/1/1917.
19. FRC 44015-006 Cooper—1889-1913.
20. FRC 44014-005/006: Letters from Uintah-Ouray—5/7/1887 and FRC 44015–006 Norris, testimony at hearing on James Frost—10/23/1905.
21. Omer C. Stewart's *Peyote Religion: A History* (Norman: University of Oklahoma Press, 1987).
22. Joseph G. Jorgensen's *The Sun Dance Religion: Power for the Powerless* (Chicago: University of Chicago Press, 1972).
23. . Marvin Opler, "The Southern Ute of Colorado" in *Acculturation in Seven American Indian Tribes,* ed. Ralph Linton (New York-London: D. Appleton-Century Company, 1940), 189-90.
24. FRC 44016-050—1925.
25. FRC 44014-005/096—6/9/1926.

Chapter 7: Categories of Change

1. Schurz, 1877.
2. FRC 44014-005/130—5/1/1878.
3. FRC 44022-202.1a—8/4/1884.
4. FRC 44016-050—l905.
5. FRC 44016-050—1921.
6. FRC 44015-006 Clay—6/26/1909.
7. FRC 44015-006 Dickinson—12/7/1917 and 12/12/1917.
8. ARCIA 1881: 23-24.
9. FRC 44014-036/006—3/15/1387.
10. FRC 44016-050—1886.
11. ARCIA 1900: 6-7.
12 FRC 44016-050—1912.

13. FRC 44016-050 —1911.
14. FRC 44015-006 Shoshoni—1918-1926 correspondence.
15. FRC 44015-006 Baker—12/31/1917.
16. FRC 44014-005/130—9/11/1877.
17. FRC 44105-005/910b—3/19/1913.
18. FRC 44014-212/006 and FRC 44084-212/250—1881-1890.
19. FRC 44105-897—1907-1917.
20. FRC 44019-161 Schnur—2/19/1925.
21. ARCIA 1880: 17.
22. ARCIA 1894: 129.
23. FRC 44014-005/130—3/14/1878 and 3/16/1878.
24. See FRC 44084-250 Subvouchers to Annuity Payrolls—1880-1899.
25. FRC 44094-005/300 Letterbook—1/3/1910.
26. FRC 44015-006 Cook, Riley—1913-1917.
27. FRC 44015-006 Moore—2/27/1918 and Clay—3/16/1926.
28. FRC 44015-006 Spencer—1913-1928.
29. FRC 44015-006 Adams, Spencer—1926-1928.
30. FRC 44015-006 Baker—1/21/1918 and 3/5/1918.
31. FRC 44015-006 Peña—6/19/1917.
32. FRC 44016-050—1913.
33. See FRC 44105-005/860—1/22/1926 for Consolidated Ute figures.
34. FRC 44017-064—11/5/1896.
35. FRC 44011-Letterbook a, pp.193-194—11/30/1900 and Letterbook d, p. 399—3/16/1907.
36. FRC 44015-006 Buck—8/27/1880.
37. FRC 44017-064—11/5/1896.
38. FRC 44016-050—1917.
39. FRC 44016-050—1920.
40. FRC 44017-154/064—3/20/1926.
41. FRC 44017-064—11/5/1896.
42. See FRC 44016-050—1916.
43. FRC 44016-050—1919.
44. FRC 44016-050—1925.
45. FRC 44011-Letterbook a, pp. 429-431—7/17/1900.
46. FRC 44010-Letterbook k, 11/9/1905.
47. FRC 44017-154/064—3/20/1926 and 3/22/1926.
48. FRC 44014-005/130—6/11/1877a.
49. See FRC 44015-006 Tree—4/26/1902 and FRC 44017-154/064—1925-1926.
50. FRC 44011-Letterbook a, pp. 392-393—10/22/1900.
51. FRC 44011-Letterbook a, pp. 458-459, 87-88, 392-393—6/2/1900, 8/8/1900, and 10/22/1900.
52. Opler, 1940: 167-168.
53. See FRC 44011-Letterbook i, pp. 484-489—6/22/1904.
54. FRC 44015-006.
55. See FRC 44105-005/806 Albuquerque—1883-1885 and 005/816—2/16/1885.

56. FRC 44016-050—1886, FRC 44014-005/130 Establishment of Schools—1885-1890 and FRC 44019-005 Mary Orr.

57. ARCIA 1895: 140.

58. FRC 44105-005/816—3/23/1897.

59. FRC 44011-Letterbook a, pp. 213-214—8/25/1900.

60. FRC 44105-005/860 Peairs—5/27/1912.

61. FRC 44105-005/806 Albuquerque—2/7/1885.

62. FRC 44019-161 Mills—2/2/1918.

63. FRC 44103-005/740—9/24/1906.

64. FRC 44015-005/816—11/6/1917.

65. FRC 44105-005/816—11/24/1917.

66. FRC 44103-052/700—4/1891.

67. FRC 44103-052/700—1/1890 and 9/30/1896.

68. FRC 44103-052/700—10/1892.

69. ARCIA 1894: 128.

70. See FRC 44014-005/175—1878-1904.

71. ARCIA 1891: 227.

72. FRC 44011-Letterbook i, pp. 484-489—6/22/1904.

73. See Stewart, 1987: 327-332.

74. FRC 44015-006 May—1925.

Chapter 8: Conclusion

1. FRC 44105-005/806 Albuquerque—2/22/1885, also FRC 44015-006 Frost—10/26/1908.

2. See FRC 44015-006 Addie Gunn—1912.

3. See FRC 44015-006 George Watts and Edna Russell.

4. FRC 44016-050—1914.

5. FRC 44015-006 William—undated, 1917.

6. FRC 44015-006 Buck—2/26/1908.

7. FRC 44015-006 Root—10/10/1921 and 12/13/1921.

8. FRC 44018-161 Abbot—7/3/1913.

9. FRC 44015-006 North—1910-1913.

10. FRC 44017-064—11/5/1896.

11. FRC 44103-005/600—3/7/1918.

12. FRC 44014-005/060—4/15/1926.

13. FRC 44017-154/064–12/8/1925.

Afterword

1. ARCIA 1891: 4.

2. Richard O. Clemmer and Omer C. Stewart, "Treaties, Reservations and Claims," in *Handbook of North American Indians, Vol 11, Great Basin*, ed. William C. Sturtevant (Washington, D.C.: Smithsonian Institution, 1986), 543.

3. Estelle Fuchs and Robert J. Havighurst, *To Live on This Earth: American Indian Education* (Garden City, N.Y.: Doubleday, 1972), 6, 8-9.

4.   Vine Deloria, Jr., *Behind the Trail of Broken Treaties* (New York: Delta, 1974), 113-160.

5.   Edward Spicer, *Cycles of Conquest* (Tucson: University of Arizona Press, 1962), 349.

6.   ARCIA 1880: 17.

7.   ARCIA 1890: 22.

8.   ARCIA 1900: 213-14, 660-61.

9.   Richard O. Clemmer, "Differential Leadership Patterns in Early Twentieth Century Great Basin Societies," *Journal of California and Great Basin Anthropology*, 11 (1989): 35-49

10.   ARCIA 1906: 404 and Kenneth R. Philp, *John Collier's Crusade for Indian Reform, 1920-1954* (Tucson: University of Arizona Press, 1977).

11.   Joseph G. Jorgensen, *The Sun Dance Religion: Power for the Powerless* (Chicago: University of Chicago Press, 1972).

12.   David F. Aberle and Omer C. Stewart, "Navaho and Ute Peyotism: A Chronological and Distributional Study," *University of Colorado Series in Anthropology No. 6.* Boulder (1957): 16-17.

13.   Katherine Marie Birmingham Osburn, "The Dawes Act, Reservation Culture and Changing Gender Roles on the Southern Ute Reservation 1887-1934" (PhD. diss., University of Denver, 1992).

14.   Robert Lowie, "Dances and Societies of the Plains Shoshone" *American Museum of Natural History Anthropological Papers* (New York) 9, no. 10 (1915).

15.   Marvin Opler, "The Southern Ute of Colorado," in *Acculturation in Seven American Indian Tribes,* ed. Ralph Linton, (New York-London: D. Appleton-Century Company, 1940), 119-203.

16.   Rupert Costo, "The Indian New Deal 1928-1945," in *Indian Self-Rule: Fifty Years under the Indian Reorganization Act*, ed. Kenneth Philp (Sun Valley, Idaho: Institute of the American West, 1983), 9.

17.   Steven I. Cornell, *The Return of the Native* (New Haven, Conn.: Yale University Press, 1988), 95; Costo, 1983: 12 and Lawrence Kelly, "The Indian Reorganization Act: The Dream and the Reality," *Pacific Historical Review* 44 (1975): 298.

18.   Lewis Meriam, *The Problem of Indian Administration* (Baltimore: Johns Hopkins University Press, 1928).

19.   Philp, 1977: 74-75.

20.   Henry F. Dobyns, "Therapeutic Experience of Responsible Democracy," in *The American Indians Today,* ed. Stuart Levine and Nancy O. Lurie, (Deland, Fla: Everett/Edwards, 1968), 268-294.

21.   Theodore Haas, *Ten Years of Tribal Government under the I.R.A.* Tribal Relations Pamphlet No. 1. (Chicago: U.S. Indian Service, 1947).

22.   U.S. Office of Indian Affairs, *Indians at Work, 1938, 7(3).*

23.   Clark Johnson, "A Study of Modern Southwestern Indian Leadership" (PhD. diss., University of Colorado, Boulder, 1963), 52.

24.   Johnson, 1963: 83.

25.   Cf. Southern Ute Tribe 1954, Southern Ute Tribe 1966; Johnson, 1963: 157-169.

26.   Cornell, 1988: 122-125.

27. Arthur V. Watkins, "Termination of Federal Supervision: The Restrictions over Indian Property and Person," *Annals of the American Academy of Political and Social Science* 311 (1957): 47-55.

28. Helen L. Peterson, "American Indian Political Participation," *Annals of the American Academy of Political and Social Sciences* 311 (1957): 118-120; William Zimmerman, Jr., "The Role of the Bureau of Indian Affairs Since 1933," *Annals of the American Academy of Political and Social Sciences* 311 (1957): 39; Jorgensen, 1972: 144-145; and Joseph G. Jorgenson, "A Century of Political and Economic Effects on American Indian Society, 1880-1990," *Journal of Ethnic Studies* 6, no. 3 (1978): 22-25.

29. Southern Ute Tribe 1954.

30. Southern Ute Tribe 1966.

31. Donald G. Callaway, Joel C. Janetski, and Omer C. Stewart, "Ute," in *Handbook of North American Indians. Vol. II Great Basin*, ed. William C. Sturtevant (Washington, D.C.: Smithsonian Institution, 1986), 361.

32. *Census of Population and Housing Characteristics, Colorado*, (Washington, D.C.: U.S. Department of Commerce, 1990), Tables 17 and 18; and Callaway et. al., 361-363.

33. Callaway et al., 1986: 358.

34. Carol B. Stack, *All Our Kin* (New York: Harper Collophon, 1974).

Bibliography

Published Government Documents

George Meston Report, see U.S. Bureau of the Census, *11th Census.*

Schurz, Carl, see U.S. Department of the Interior, *Report of the Secretary of the Interior.*

U.S. Bureau of the Census, *11th Census, Report on Indians Taxed and Not Taxed. (George Meston Report),* Washington, D.C: Government Printing Office, 1890.

——. *Census of Population and Housing Characteristics, Colorado*, Washington, D.C.: U.S. Department of Commerce, 1990.

U.S. Congress. House. H. R. Committee Reports, *House Committee Report, Number 1205*, 52d Congress, 1st Session, Washington, D.C: Government Printing Office, 1892.

——. *Report of House Committee on Indian Affairs (Mr. Hunter),* to accompany H.R. 6742, 53d Congress, 2d Session, Washington, D.C: Government Printing Office, 1894.

U.S. Department of the Interior. *Annual Report of the Commissioner of Indian Affairs*, Washington, D.C: Government Printing Office, 1877, 1880, 1890, 1893, 1896, 1897, 1899, and 1900.

——. *Report of the Secretary of the Interior*, Washington, D.C: Government Printing Office, 1877.

U.S. Congress. Senate. *Senate Report, Number 836,* 49th Congress, 1st Session, Washington, D.C: Government Printing Office, 1886.

——. *Report of Southern Ute Commission, 1889*: Report of Chairman, Secretary's Journal and Commissioner J. J. Enright's Report on Agreement with Southern Utes, Sen. Exec. Doc., 50th Congress, 2d Session, Washington, D.C: Government Printing Office, 1889.

Unpublished Government Documents

Records of Southern Ute Agency, 1877-1952, National Archives No. RG 75. Federal Records Center, Denver, Colorado.

Tri-Ethnic Microfilm Roll #6, *Federal Records Center Roll V*, University of Colorado, Library, Western History Section.

Southern Ute Tribal Documents

Long-Range Rehabilitation Plan to Govern the Seven Million Dollar Land Claim Settlement of 1950. Washington, D.C.: U.S. Congress, 1954.

Southern Ute Rehabilitation Plan. Ignacio, CO, 1956.

Progress Report, Southern Ute Rehabilitation Plan. Ms., 1958.

Where We Stand. Ignacio, CO, 1960.

Ten Year Planning Report. Ignacio, CO, 1964.

Progress and Future: A Report by the Southern Ute Tribe, Dallas, TX: Taylor Publishing Co. Ignacio, CO, 1966.

Tri-Ethnic Steering Committee: Southern Ute Community Master Plan, Ms. 1968.

Comprehensive Plan of the Southern Ute Tribe. Ignacio, CO, 1974.

Historical and Anthropological Studies

Aberle, David F., and Omer C. Stewart, "Navaho and Ute Peyotism: A Chronological and Distributional Study." *University of Colorado Series in Anthropology No. 6.* Boulder, 1957.

Callaway, Donald G., Joel C. Janetski, and Omer C. Stewart, "Ute." Pp. 336-367 in *Handbook of North American Indians. Vol. 2 Great Basin,* ed. William C. Sturtevant. Washington, D.C.: Smithsonian Institution, 1986.

Clemmer, Richard O., "Differential Leadership Patterns in Early Twentieth Century Great Basin Societies," *Journal of California and Great Basin Anthropology,* 11 (1989): 35-49.

Clemmer, Richard O., and Omer C. Stewart, "Treaties, Reservations and Claims." Pp. 525-557 in *Handbook of North American Indians, Vol 2, Great Basin,* ed. William C. Sturtevant. Washington, D.C.: Smithsonian Institution, 1986.

Cornell, Steven I., *The Return of the Native.* New Haven: Yale University Press, 1988.

Costo, Rupert, "The Indian New Deal 1928-1945." Pp. 10-14 In *Indian Self-Rule: Fifty Years Under the Indian Reorganization Act,* ed. Kenneth Philp. Sun Valley, Idaho: Institute of the American West, 1983.

——, "Federal Indian Policy." Pp. 48-54 in *Indian Self-Rule: Fifty Years Under the Indian Reorganization Act,* edited by Kenneth Philp. Salt Lake City: Sun Valley, Idaho: Institute of the American West, 1983.

Deloria, Vine, Jr., *Behind the Trail of Broken Treaties.* New York: Delta, 1974.

Dobyns, Henry F., "Therapeutic Experience of Responsible Democracy." Pp. 268-294 in *The American Indians Today,* ed. by Stuart Levine and Nancy O. Lurie, Deland, FL: Everett/Edwards, 1968.

Fuchs, Estelle, and Robert J. Havighurst, *To Live on This Earth: American Indian Education.* Garden City, NY: Doubleday, 1972.

Haas, Theodore, "Ten Years of Tribal Government Under the I.R.A." Tribal Relations Pamphlet No. 1., Chicago: U.S. Indian Service, 1947.

Herskovits, Melville, *Acculturation.* Gloucester: Peter Smith, 1938.

Indians at Work, see U.S. Office of Indian Affairs, below.

Jefferson, James, Robert W. Delaney, and Gregory C. Thompson, *The Southern Utes: A Tribal History.* Salt Lake City: University of Utah Press, 1972.

Johnson, Clark, "A Study of Modern Southwestern Indian Leadership." PhD diss., University of Colorado, Boulder, 1963.

Jorgensen, Joseph G., *The Sun Dance Religion: Power for the Powerless.* Chicago: University of Chicago Press, 1972.

——, "A Century of Political and Economic Effects on American Indian Society, 1880-1990," *Journal of Ethnic Studies* 6, no. 3 (1978): 1-82.

Kelly, Lawrence, "The Indian Reorganization Act: The Dream and the Reality," *Pacific Historical Review* 44 (1975): 291-312.

Lewis, Meriam, *The Problem of Indian Administration.* Baltimore: Johns Hopkins University Press, 1928.

Lowie, Robert, "Dances and Societies of the Plains Shoshone," *American Museum of Natural History Anthropological Papers* 9, no. 10 (1915).

Opler, Marvin, "The Southern Ute of Colorado." Pp. 119-203 in *Acculturation in Seven American Indian Tribes,* ed. by Ralph Linton. New York-London: D. Appleton-Century Company, 1940.

Osburn, Katherine Marie Birmingham, *The Dawes Act, Reservation Culture and Changing Gender Roles on the Southern Ute Reservation 1887-1934.* Ph.D. diss., University of Denver, 1992.

Peterson, Helen L., "American Indian Political Participation." *Annals of the American Academy of Political and Social Sciences* 311 (1957): 116-126.

Philp, Kenneth R., *John Collier's Crusade for Indian Reform, 1920-1954.* Tucson: University of Arizona Press, 1977.

Quintana, Frances L., *Pobladores. Hispanic Americans of the Ute Frontier.* Aztec: Frances Leon Quintana, 1991.

Spicer, Edward, "Yaqui Religious Acculturation," *American Anthropologist* 60 (1958): 433-441.

——, *Cycles of Conquest.* Tucson: University of Arizona Press, 1962.

Stack, Carol B., *All Our Kin.* New York: Harper Collophon, 1974.

Stewart, Omer C., *Ute Indians: Before and After White Contact.* Publ. 56, Institute of Behavioral Science at Boulder, University of Colorado, Boulder: University of Colorado Press, 1966.

——, *Ethnohistorical Bibliography of the Ute Indians of Colorado.* Boulder: University of Colorado Press, 1971.

——, *Peyote Religion: A History.* Norman: University of Oklahoma Press, 1987.

Swadesh, Frances L., "Analysis of Records of the Southern Ute Agency, 1877 through 1952." Appendix A in Omer C. Stewart, *Ethnohistorical Bibliography of the Ute Indians of Colorado.* Boulder: University of Colorado Press, 1971.

——, *Los Primeros Pobladores. Hispanic Americans of the Ute Frontier.* Notre Dame: University of Notre Dame Press, 1974.

U.S. Office of Indian Affairs, *Indians at Work 7(3).* Washington, D.C.: U.S. Office of Indian Affairs, 1938.

Watkins, Arthur V., "Termination of Federal Supervision: The Restrictions over Indian Property and Person," *Annals of the American Academy of Political and Social Science* 311 (1957): 47-55.

Zimmerman, William, Jr., "The Role of the Bureau of Indian Affairs Since 1933." *Annals of the American Academy of Political and Social Sciences* 311 (1957): 31-40.

Index

Indian names are italicized.

About the Authors

Frances Leon Quintana was educated at the Ecole Internationale de Geneve and Vassar College, from which she received her B.A. in 1938. Winning a scholarship to Yale, she was privileged to study briefly under Professor Edward Sapir. She received her M.A. in 1962 and her Ph.D. in 1966 from the University of Colorado at Boulder, where she studied under Professor Omer C. Stewart. It was at this time that she became acquainted with the Ignacio area, performing fieldwork with the Tri-Ethnic Project. From 1968-1978, she served as Curator of Ethnology at the Laboratory of Anthropology of the Museum of New Mexico, where she specialized in the ethnology and ethnohistory of Hispanic communities. Her book *Los Primeros Pobladores: Hispanic Americans of the Ute Frontier* was published in 1974 and re-issued in a second edition in 1991 as *Pobladores: Hispanic Americans of the Ute Frontier.* That volume is available through Ganados del Valle, PO Box 118 Los Ojos, NM 87551.

Richard O. Clemmer is professor of anthropology at University of Denver. He did social and economic research among the Southern Utes as a Tribal employee from 1981 to 1983. He is author of *Roads in the Sky: The Hopi Indians in a Century of Change* and editor, with L. Daniel Myers and Mary Elizabeth Rudden, of *Julian Steward and the Great Basin: The Making of an Anthropologist.*